KEYS TO WOODY PLANTS

THE LEAVES OF POISON IVY AND POISON SUMAC AND SOME HARMLESS PLANTS WITH WHICH THEY
ARE OFTEN CONFUSED

1, Poison ivy, *Rhus Toxicodendron* L. Petiole bearing three leaflets; buds visible. 2, Virginia creeper, *Parthenocissus quinquefolia* (L). Planch. Petiole bearing five leaflets. 3, Silky dogwood, *Cornus Amomum* Mill. Leaves opposite, simple. 4, Fragrant sumac, *Rhus aromatica* Ait. Petiole bearing three leaflets: buds hidden under base of petiole. 5, Poison sumac, *Rhus Vernix* L. Leaves alternate: petiole bearing several leaflets with entire margins: buds visible in the axils. 6, Dwarf sumac, *Rhus copallina* L. Margin of leaflets entire or toothed, leaf axis winged. 7, Smooth sumac, *Rhus glabra* L. Margin of leaflets serrate, buds hidden under base of petiole. 8. Staghorn sumac, *Rhus typhina* L. Like 7, but with hairy leaves and twigs. 9, Mountain ash, *Pyrus americana* DC. Margin of leaflets serrate: buds visible. 10, Black ash, *Fraxinus nigra* Marsh. Leaves and buds opposite. 11, Elderberry, *Sambucus canadensis* L. Leaves and buds opposite. (After Muenscher, in *Cornell University Experiment Station Extension Bulletin 191*.)

KEYS TO
WOODY PLANTS

W. C. MUENSCHER

SIXTH EDITION, *REVISED*

Comstock Publishing Associates

A DIVISION OF

CORNELL UNIVERSITY PRESS

ITHACA AND LONDON

First edition, July, 1922
Second edition, July, 1926
Third edition, July, 1930
Fourth edition, March, 1936
Fifth edition, June, 1946
Sixth edition, May, 1950

First printing, Cornell Paperbacks, 1992

International Standard Book Number 0-8014-0307-3

PRINTED IN THE UNITED STATES OF AMERICA

Cornell University Press strives to use environmentally responsible
suppliers and materials to the fullest extent possible in the publishing
of its books. Such materials include vegetable-based, low-VOC inks
and acid-free papers that are recycled, totally chlorine-free, or partly
composed of nonwood fibers.

Cloth printing

15   17   19   20   18   16   14

Paperback printing

5   7   9   10   8   6   4

PREFACE

A woodsman or farmer from practical experience usually recognizes by general appearances or by certain "ear marks" the common trees and a few shrubs of the region with which he is familiar. But take him out of this region and place him among different trees and his familiarity with general appearances will be of little value to him in trying to identify his new tree friends either with or without the aid of a book. The reason is twofold. First, it is very difficult to describe and incorporate general appearances in descriptions of plants, and second it therefore follows that usually the best books on trees are written in the terminology of systematic botany which is often too technical for the average person who is or who should be interested in the woody plants around him. The student of systematic botany on the other hand must depend to a large extent upon the floral structure and arrangement in his descriptions of plants and is often puzzled when asked to identify a plant when it is not in flower or when it is in a leafless condition, because of a lack of knowledge of general appearances.

The purpose of this little guide is twofold: first, to aid the beginner in identifying some of the more common woody plants in the summer or winter condition, and second, to familiarize the student with descriptive terms and the use of keys and teach him how and what to look for when examining a woody plant, or a part of it, with a view to its identification. It is hoped that the beginner who has been able to use this guide with a reasonable degree of success will have acquired sufficient skill in the use of keys and the observation of diagnostic characteristics of woody plants in the summer or winter condition to enable him, with the aid of more comprehensive works, to identify practically all the woody plants desired.

In these keys the aim has been to point out, as far as possible, diagnostic field characteristics, exclusive of flowers. The summer keys are based primarily upon leaves and fruits; the winter keys are based primarily upon bud and twig characters, supplemented by those of bark, general habits, and fruits.

In the preparation of these keys the writer has made free use of every available source of information. Although he has referred to many manuals and books on trees and shrubs, the keys are based upon actual study of the woody flora about Cornell University and other regions. Every species included in the keys has been studied from living material.

W. C. M.

July, 1922.

NOTE TO THE SECOND EDITION

The keys here presented have been somewhat rearranged from the first edition. About 40 genera and 160 species have been added. In the preparation of these keys the writer has received valued assistance and suggestions from his colleagues and the users of the first edition of the keys: Dr. A. S. Foster who had access to the library and collections of the Arnold Arboretum and prepared some of the keys to species, checked many of the keys with living material, and looked up certain nomenclatorial questions; the members of the staff of the Arnold Arboretum who extended assistance and courtesies to Dr. Foster; Dr. W. E. Manning who prepared the keys to *Cornus,* and also checked many of the keys with living material; Professor K. M. Wiegand and Professor A. J. Eames who gave permission to include foliage keys to *Amelanchier* and *Salix* prepared by them; Minnie Worthen Muenscher who gave much assistance throughout the preparation and proof reading of the keys. The writer wishes to express his appreciation and thanks to all who have helped.

July 1, 1926

NOTE TO THE SIXTH EDITION

In the present edition a number of rearrangements and corrections have been made in the keys. A few species have been added and a number of nomenclatorial changes, indicated as a result of recent studies of taxonomists, have been introduced. Citations to pages for keys to species have been inserted after the generic names in the genus keys. The reference list has been expanded by the inclusion of the more recent publications on woody plants.

Acknowledgment is here made of the interest expressed by, and the helpful suggestions received from, many former students and other users of the previous editions of these "Keys." These suggestions have been appreciated and were helpful in the preparation of the present revision. Not all who made suggestions can be mentioned here but acknowledgments for special assistance are extended to Dr. Robert T. Clausen and Dr. Babette I. Brown. Finally, thanks are due to Mr. Victor Reynolds, manager of the Comstock Publishing Company, for his interest and cooperation in expediting the publication of the present edition.

W. C. M.

January, 1950

TABLE OF CONTENTS

INTRODUCTION

The following notes are given in order to facilitate the use of the keys presented in this guide.

The keys are based upon the common native woody plants of the northeastern United States. Most species having only a very local distribution within this area have been omitted. A few of the commonly planted exotics of the same region are included. In all, about 160 genera and approximately 500 species have been included.

In the key to genera the main divisions are based upon the presence or absence of leaves. Those species on which some leaves remain over winter (most of the conifers and "broad-leaved evergreens") occur only in the first main division of the key. Keys for identifying species have been provided for all genera except *Crataegus* and *Rosa*. For most of the larger genera both "summer" and "winter" keys to species have been provided.

All the keys are strictly dichotomous. The two coordinate leads always bear the same index number. The subordinate leads under the main leads are numbered and indented consecutively. If there is no further subdivision the name of the genus or species appears.

In using the keys here presented it must be kept in mind that they are based upon the woody plants as they grow in the field. To be sure, it is not always possible or necessary to have access to the whole plant, but the specimens selected for tracing through the key should represent normal structures from well grown individuals. Small seedlings, sucker shoots and coppice growth frequently produce twigs, leaves and buds quite unlike those developed by normal growth of more mature individuals. Such specimens may give some difficulty in the keys. The color of the bark on young stems is subject to considerable variation. When color of twigs is mentioned it refers to winter color of the shoots of the last season's growth; the bark on the older shoots (branchlets) may be quite different in color and texture. The color stated for fruits refers to that of the ripe fruits. On twigs with no terminal bud the uppermost lateral bud frequently appears terminal (pseudo-terminal bud). Such buds have a leaf-scar on one side and an abscission scar from the growing point on the opposite side usually somewhat raised on a short stub. The persistent or "evergreen" nature of leaves may be determined in summer by the presence of leaves on the growth of the previous season, that is, on the axis below or behind the bud-scars.

The nomenclature used is in accord with the rules adopted by the International Congress of Botanists in Vienna in 1905 and subsequent congresses. In the keys, only the scientific names are given, but a complete list of all species included in the keys is appended for reference and in this list each scientific name is generally followed by a common name in rather general use. In cases where a plant appears under a name not employed in the common manuals, it is followed by one or more synonyms in parenthesis. In this list the orders and families follow the systematic arrangement of Engler and Prantl; the genera are arranged essentially as in Gray's Manual; the species are arranged alphabetically.

A. KEYS TO GENERA

KEY TO THE GROUPS OF PLANTS

I. PLANTS WITH NEEDLE-LIKE, SCALE-LIKE, OR AWL-SHAPED LEAVES

(Includes conifers and a few small heath-like shrubs.)

1. Trees or erect or ascending shrubs, 1 meter or more high.
  2. Leaves alternate or in fascicles or clusters (not opposite or whorled), needle-like, (scale-like leaves often present on fruiting branches of *Taxodium*); fruit a cone.
    3. Leaves in fascicles of 2–5 leaves or mostly in clusters of many leaves on spur-like branches.
      4. Leaves in fascicles of 2–5 leaves, persistent ....**Pinus p. 59** *
      4. Leaves mostly in clusters of many leaves on the ends of spur-like branches, deciduous ....**Larix p. 55**
    3. Leaves scattered, alternate.
      5. Ultimate twigs very slender, greenish and mostly deciduous; leaves deciduous, yellowish-green, much flattened and in two ranks; bark fibrous; cones with several wedge-shaped woody scales.
                                         Taxodium distichum
      5. Ultimate twigs not deciduous; leaves persistent, not yellowish-green above; bark not fibrous.
        6. Branchlets roughened by the persistent leaf bases; leaves deciduous when dry; cones pendulous, the bracts shorter than the cone scales.
          7. Leaves sessile, mostly four-sided, often sharp-pointed ....**Picea p. 58**
          7. Leaves stalked, flattened, blunt ....**Tsuga canadensis**

---

* The page citations refer to the key to species or systematic list.

 6. Branchlets not roughened by persistent leaf bases.
　　8. Leaves sessile, flattened, (seldom four-sided); leaf-scars orbicular, not decurrent; cones erect, the scales deciduous ....**Abies p. 41**
　　8. Leaves stalked, flattened; leaf-scars decurrent.
　　　9. Leaves mostly with obtuse tips and with two white lines on the lower surface; cones pendulous, the scales persistent in the axils of long exserted bracts ....**Pseudotsuga taxifolia**
　　　9. Leaves with acute tips, yellow-green on the lower surface; "fruit" drupe-like ....**Taxus p. 73**
 2. Leaves opposite or whorled, often of two kinds, scale-like, awl-shaped, or linear.
　　10. Leaves in whorls of 20–30, linear, each consisting of 2 connate leaves, 8–12 cm. long ....**Sciadopitys verticillata**
　　10. Leaves not as above.
　　　(See key to Cupressaceae on p. 50.)
　　　11. Leaves in whorls of four; cones elongated ....**Libocedrus decurrens**
　　　11. Leaves opposite or in whorls of three.
　　　　12. Fruit berry-like ....**Juniperus p. 50**
　　　　12. Fruit a cone.
　　　　　13. Cones subglobose, scales peltate ....**Chamaecyparis p. 50**
　　　　　13. Cones elongated, scales not peltate ....**Thuja p. 50**
 1. Low, prostrate or creeping shrubs or mats, 1–10 dm. high.
　　14. Leaves opposite, scale-like or minute.
　　　15. Stems erect; leaves sagittate ....**Calluna vulgaris**
　　　15. Stems creeping; leaves not sagittate ....**Juniperus horizontalis**
　　14. Leaves alternate; stems forming low mats.
　　　16. Leaves covered with downy hairs ....**Hudsonia p. 53**
　　　16. Leaves glabrous or nearly so.
　　　　17. Margin of leaves revolute; leaves falsely whorled, 4–7 mm. long; leaf-scars decurrent; fruit a drupe.
　　　　　18. Margin of leaves denticulate ....**Corema Conradii**
　　　　　18. Margin of leaves entire ....**Empetrum nigrum**
　　　　17. Margin of leaves not revolute.
　　　　　19. Leaves imbricated, subulate, 2–4 mm. long; leaf-scars not decurrent; fruit a capsule ....**Cassiope hypnoides**
　　　　　19. Leaves not imbricated, linear, acute, 5–20 mm. long; leaf-scars decurrent.
　　　　　　20. Apex of leaf sharp-pointed; "fruit" drupe-like, red.
　　　　　　　　　　　　　　　　　　　　　　　　　　Taxus canadensis
　　　　　　20. Apex of leaf blunt; fruit a capsule ....**Phyllodoce coerulea**

II. PLANTS WITH OPPOSITE OR WHORLED SIMPLE LEAVES

1. Leaves lobed.
   2. Leaves palmately lobed.
      3. Leaf blades less than 20 cm. long.
         4. Petioles with stipules and glands, or if without glands, the lower surface of leaf densely pubescent; fruit a drupe . . . . . . **Viburnum p. 74**
         4. Petioles without stipules and glands, or if stipules are present, the lower surface of leaf not densely hairy; fruit a samara . . . . **Acer p. 41**
      3. Leaf blades more than 20 cm. long.
         5. Leaves with long tapering tip, not velvety, usually in whorls of three; pith continuous; fruit a long capsule . . . . **Catalpa p. 47**
         5. Leaves with obtuse or rounded tip, velvety, always opposite; pith chambered or hollow; fruit an ovate capsule . . . **Paulownia tomentosa**
   2. Leaves pinnately lobed (often many leaves are not lobed at all).
      6. Margin of lobes entire; sap watery; low shrubs; fruit a berry.
         Symphoricarpos p. 73
      6. Margin of lobes serrate; sap milky; trees; fruit a head of achenes.
         Broussonetia papyrifera
1. Leaves not lobed.
   7. Stems climbing, creeping, prostrate, or forming low mats.
      8. Stems climbing; leaves deciduous or persisting; vines.
         9. Aerial rootlets present on stems; fruit a capsule.
            10. Leaves deciduous or persistent; branchlets brown.
               Decumaria barbara
            10. Leaves persistent; branchlets green . . . . **Evonymus fortunei**
         9. Aerial rootlets absent; leaves persistent, or if deciduous, then the uppermost often connate and glaucous; fruit a berry . . . . **Lonicera p. 55**
      8. Stems prostrate, creeping, or forming low mats; (often only slightly woody); leaves persisting.
         10a. Leaves entire or slightly undulate; plants creeping or prostrate; fruit a berry or follicle.
            11. Leaves with pellucid dots . . . . **Ascyrum p. 44**
            11. Leaves without pellucid dots.
               12. Leaves and young stems strongly pubescent; fruit a black berry.
                  Lonicera japonica
               12. Leaves and stems glabrous or nearly so.
                  13. Leaf base cordate or rounded; fruit a red berry . . **Mitchella repens**
                  13. Leaf base narrow or cuneate.
                     14. Leaves over 2 cm. long, not revolute; stems slightly woody, creeping; fruit a follicle . . . . **Vinca minor**
                     14. Leaves less than 1 cm. long, revolute; stems woody, forming dense low mats; fruit a capsule . . . **Loiseleuria procumbens**
         10a. Leaves crenate or serrate; plants creeping or erect; fruit a capsule.

15. Leaves rounded-oval, crenate; branches brownish pubescent; stems slender and creeping .... **Linnaea borealis**
15. Leaves oblanceolate, sharply serrate; branches glabrous.
  16. Leaves opposite; stems with longitudinal ridges, stoloniferous.

Evonymus p. 51
  16. Leaves in false whorls; stems erect, from creeping rootstocks.

Chimaphila p. 47
7. Stems erect; trees or shrubs.
  17. Margin of leaves entire.
    18. Leaf blade 15–50 cm. long, ovate with cordate, subcordate, or truncate base.
      19. Leaves with long-tapering tip, not velvety, usually in whorls; pith continuous; fruit a long capsule .... **Catalpa p. 47**
      19. Leaves with obtuse or rounded tip, velvety, opposite; pith chambered or hollow; fruit an ovate capsule .... **Paulownia tomentosa**
    18. Leaf blade less than 15 cm. long or else not ovate.
      20. Leaves and twigs spicy-aromatic .... **Calycanthus p. 45**
      20. Leaves and twigs not spicy-aromatic.
        21. Leaves and twigs covered with silvery or rusty scales. **Shepherdia p. 72**
        21. Leaves and twigs not covered with silvery or rusty scales.
          22. Leaves ovate with cordate, subcordate, or truncate base and long-tapering tip .... **Syringa vulgaris**
          22. Leaves not with the above combination of characteristics, (base acute, or if cordate, the tip not long-tapering).
            23. Leaves 1 cm. long or shorter; (low shrub with coriaceous, persistent leaves) .... **Leiophyllum buxifolium**
            23. Leaves more than 2 cm. long.
              24. Leaves with pellucid dots; (low shrubs with short, leafy shoots in axils of leaves); fruit a capsule ..... **Hypericum p. 53**
              24. Leaves without pellucid dots.
                25. Branchlets quadrangular, flattened, or winged; leaves sessile or nearly so, leathery, persistent.
                  26. Lower surface of leaves glaucous, margin strongly revolute; twigs flattened; fruit a 5-valved capsule.

Kalmia polifolia
                  26. Lower surface of leaves light green with median white band, margin only slightly revolute; twigs quadrangular or winged; fruit a three-valved capsule.

Buxus sempervirens
                25. Branchlets neither quadrangular, flattened, nor winged; leaves with distinct petioles.
                  27. Leaves tending to be crowded toward the end of the season's growth, often in whorls of three, leathery, persistent; fruit a capsule .... **Kalmia p. 55**

27.   Leaves scattered in pairs along the season's growth, deciduous.
> 28.   Lateral buds imbedded in the bark, supra-axillary; leaves often in whorls of three; fruit a head of nutlets . . . . **Cephalanthus occidentalis**
> 28.   Lateral buds axillary, not imbedded in the bark; leaves opposite.
>> 29.   Bark of stems and branches loose, peeling off in long, shreddy pieces: fruit a berry.
>>> 30.   Twigs closely branched, very slender; bundle-scar one.
>>> **Symphoricarpos** p. 73
>>> 30.   Twigs not closely branched, of medium thickness; bundle-scars three; bud-scales often persisting at base of twigs . . . . **Lonicera** p. 55
>> 29.   Bark of stems and older branches smooth, not peeling off in long shreds.
>>> 31.   Leaves with lateral veins running somewhat parallel with the margin and meeting near the apex; fruit a drupe . . . . **Cornus** p. 48
>>> 31.   Leaves with lateral veins ending near the margin and not running to the apex.
>>>> 32.   Lower surface of leaf, especially along the midrib, scurfy, rusty-brown, woolly or glandular, (margin of leaf often finely serrate); fruit a drupe . . . . **Viburnum** p. 74
>>>> 32.   Lower surface of leaf not as above.
>>>>> 33.   Leaf blade 1–6 cm. long, glabrate; twigs glabrous or puberulent; fruit a berry . . . . **Ligustrum** p. 55
>>>>> 33.   Leaf blade 7–25 cm. long, usually pubescent on lower surface; twigs often pubescent; fruit a drupe . . . . . **Chionanthus virginica**

17.   Margin of leaves not entire, usually serrate or dentate.
> 34.   Petiole bases of opposite leaves joined by a distinct transverse line or meeting.
>> 35.   Buds imbedded under the petiole base, not axillary; fruit a capsule.
>> **Philadelphus** p. 58
>> 35.   Buds not imbedded, axillary.
>>> 36.   Leaves with yellow, glandular dots; twigs strongly striated.
>>> **Iva frutescens**
>>> 36.   Leaves without yellow, glandular dots; twigs not strongly striated.
>>>> 37.   Decurrent, ciliate ridge from transverse line connecting petiole bases present; fruit a capsule . . . . **Diervilla Lonicera**
>>>> 37.   Decurrent ridge, as above, absent.
>>>>> 38.   Buds naked or covered with valvate scales . . . . **Viburnum** p. 74
>>>>> 38.   Buds covered with imbricated scales.
>>>>>> 39.   Leaves closely and finely doubly serrate; stipules present; leaf-scars ciliate; fruit a cluster of shiny black nutlets surrounded by a large, persistent calyx . . . . **Rhodotypos kerrioides**
>>>>>> 39.   Leaves simply dentate or serrate; stipules absent or apparently so; leaf-scars not ciliate.

40. Bud-scales from buds of previous year persisting; petiole usually longer than the blade; fruit a capsule......................**Hydrangea** p. 53
40. Bud-scales from previous year not persisting; petiole shorter than the blade; fruit a drupe ....**Viburnum** p. 74
34. Petiole bases of opposite leaves not joined by a distinct transverse line, not meeting.
  41. Some of the twigs and branchlets ending in sharp black spines; inner bark yellow and bitter; fruit a dark berry ....**Rhamnus cathartica**
  41. Twigs and bark not as above.
    42. Pith hollow or chambered, not continuous between the nodes; fruit a capsule ....**Forsythia** p. 52
    42. Pith continuous or spongy between the nodes, (rarely chambered in *Evonymus*).
      43. Leaves persistent, nearly sessile; low shrubs; fruit a capsule.
        44. Branchlets green; pith greenish or white; seeds red ..**Evonymus** p. 51
        44. Branchlets gray-brown; pith brown; seeds white.

Pachistima Canbyi

      43. Leaves deciduous.
        45. Leaves woolly on lower surface; petiole very short; branchlets gray-brown; fruit berry-like ....**Callicarpa americana**
        45. Leaves not woolly on lower surface; petiole long; branchlets green or reddish-purple; fruit a capsule.
          46. Bud-scales several; petioles long ....**Evonymus** p. 51
          46. Bud-scale one; petioles short ....**Salix purpurea**

III. PLANTS WITH OPPOSITE COMPOUND LEAVES

1. Leaves with three or fewer leaflets.
   2. Leaflets two; (a vine with branched tendrils); fruit a capsule.

      Bignonia capreolata
   2. Leaflets three.
      3. Stems climbing or twining; vines; fruit a hairy achene . . . . .**Clematis** p. 47
      3. Stems not climbing or twining, (sometimes pendulous in *Forsythia*); trees or shrubs.
         4. Petioles long; leaflets of nearly equal size; older bark white-striped; fruit a bladder-like inflated capsule . . . . **Staphylea trifolia**
         4. Petioles short; lateral leaflets reduced or mostly absent; bark not white-striped; capsule not inflated . . . .**Forsythia** p. 52
1. Leaves with more than three leaflets.
   5. Leaves palmately compound; leaflets 5–7; fruit a three-valved capsule with nut-like seeds . . . .**Aesculus** p. 42
   5. Leaves pinnately compound.
      6. Stems climbing, with aerial rootlets; vines; leaflets 7–11, ovate-lanceolate, with serrate margin; fruit a fusiform, two-celled capsule. .**Campsis radicans**
      6. Stems not climbing; erect trees or shrubs.
         7. Pith very large; bark with large, raised, corky lenticels; fruit berry-like.

            Sambucus p. 72
         7. Pith small; lenticels not conspicuously raised; fruit a samara.
            8. Leaflets mostly 3–5, lobed or coarsely serrate; twigs often glaucous.

               Acer Negundo
            8. Leaflets mostly 5–11, entire or finely serrate; twigs not glaucous.

               Fraxinus p. 52

IV. PLANTS WITH ALTERNATE SIMPLE LEAVES

(Sometimes some of the leaves are clustered on short spurs.)

1. Leaves lobed.
   2. Stems climbing or twining; vines.
      3. Leaves with one or more lateral lobes on each side of midrib; leaves and stems with rank odor when crushed; fruit a red berry. **Solanum dulcamara**
      3. Leaves palmately-lobed and -veined.
         4. Aerial rootlets present on twigs and branchlets; leaves persistent, lobes mostly entire; veins whitish on upper surface of leaves.
            Hedera Helix
         4. Aerial rootlets absent; lobes mostly serrate, veins not whitish; fruit a berry or drupe.
            5. Tendrils present; fruit a berry.
               5a. Ends of tendrils provided with disc-like appendages.
                  Parthenocissus tricuspidata
               5a. Ends of tendrils without disc-like appendages, coiled . . . . **Vitis p. 76**
            5. Tendrils absent; fruit a drupe.
               6. Petiole 1–4 cm. long; the middle lobe longer than the lateral ones; leaves pubescent; drupe red . . . . **Cocculus carolinus**
               6. Petiole 5–15 cm. long; the lobes nearly equal in length; mature leaves glabrous or nearly so.
                  6a. Leaves peltate near the edge; lobes rounded; drupe blue.
                     Menispermum canadense
                  6a. Leaves cordate at base; lobes acuminate; drupe black.
                     Calycocarpum Lyoni
   2. Stems erect or prostrate; trees or shrubs.
      7. Leaves broadly fan-shaped with more or less dichotomously branched veins running to the margin, bluntly two-lobed, mostly on short spur-like branches; fruit drupe-like; gymnosperms . . . . **Ginkgo biloba**
      7. Leaves and veins not as above; angiosperms.
         8. Leaves distinctly palmately-lobed and -veined.
            9. Plants with milky sap . . . . **Ficus carica**
            9. Plants without milky sap.
               10. Leaves star-shaped, 5–7 lobed, with evenly serrate margins; branches often with corky ridges; fruit a long-stalked, spherical head of capsules . . . . **Liquidambar styraciflua**
               10. Leaves not star-shaped, 3–5 lobed, the margins not evenly serrate.
                  11. Base of petiole hollow, forming a hood over the lateral bud; stipules or scars prominent; bark of trunk and branches peeling off in large plates; fruit a suspended ball of hairy achenes . . . . **Platanus p. 60**

11.   Base of petiole not hollow; lateral buds axillary; stipules inconspicuous or absent.
   12.   Younger branches and lower surface of leaves white-tomentose.
                          Populus p. 60
   12.   Younger branches and lower surface of leaves not white-tomentose.
      13.   Older bark separating in numerous thin layers; spines absent.
         14.   Leaves and twigs glandular-clammy; fruit aggregate, berry-like.
                          Rubus odoratus
         14.   Leaves and twigs not glandular-clammy; fruit an inflated pod.
                          Physocarpus opulifolius
      13.   Older bark close, not separating in layers.
         15.   Leaf base cuneate; stipules or stipule-scars present; spines absent; fruit a capsule ....**Hibiscus syriacus**
         15.   Leaf base cordate or if cuneate, stipules absent or adnate to the petiole; spines often present; fruit a berry ....**Ribes p. 68**
8. Leaves pinnately-lobed or at least not distinctly palmately-lobed, (except sometimes in *Sassafras*).
   16.   Leaves with three main veins from near the base, mostly with one or a few lateral lobes.
      17.   Lobes entire; leaves spicy-aromatic; bark of branchlets smooth and green; fruit a blue drupe ....**Sassafras albidum**
      17.   Lobes serrate; leaves not spicy-aromatic; bark of branchlets not green.
         18.   Sap milky; lobes rounded or pointed; thorns absent; fruit multiple.
            19.   Leaves velvety on lower surface; petioles 5–10 cm. long; twigs velvety ....**Broussonetia papyrifera**
            19.   Leaves not velvety on lower surface; petioles usually 2–4 cm. long; twigs not velvety ....**Morus p. 57**
         18.   Sap not milky; lobes pointed; thorns usually present; fruit a pome.
                         Pyrus p. 77
   16.   Leaves with one large main vein (midrib), lobed variously.
      20.   Leaves pinnately-lobed.
         21.   Leaves with numerous deep, rounded lobes on each side of the midrib, sweet-scented; shrubs; fruit small, nut-like ....**Myrica peregrina**
         21.   Leaves with few to several rounded or pointed lobes on each side of the midrib, not sweet-scented.
            22.   Leaves 10–20 cm. long; buds clustered at the end of twigs; fruit an acorn ....**Quercus p. 63**
            22.   Leaves 4–10 cm. long; buds not clustered at the end of twigs; fruit a small pome; thorns often present ....**Crataegus p. 83**
      20.   Leaves not pinnately-lobed.
         23.   Leaves with truncate apex, and two broad lateral lobes on each side of midrib; buds covered by membranous stipules.
                         Liriodendron tulipifera
         23.   Leaves not truncate, irregularly lobed; buds scaly ....**Crataegus p. 83**

1. Leaves not lobed.
  24. Margin of leaves entire.
    25. Leaves usually with a pair of tendrils at the base of petiole; stem bundles scattered; spines or prickles usually present; stem usually green and climbing; fruit a blue, black or red berry ....Smilax p. 72
    25. Leaves without tendrils at base of petiole; stem bundles in a ring in cross section.
      26. Leaves persistent, coriaceous, and often revolute.
        27. Stems climbing, creeping, prostrate, or forming dense low mats.
        27a. Stems climbing ....Cocculus carolinus
        27a. Stems not climbing.
          28. Stems covered with brown hairs, prostrate or creeping.
            29. Leaves .5–1.5 cm. long, with coarse, brown, scale-like hairs on lower surface; fruit a white berry ....Chiogenes hispidula
            29. Leaves 2–8 cm. long, oval-oblong, rugose, glabrous; fruit a capsule ....Epigaea repens
          28. Stems not covered with brown hairs.
            30. Twigs and petioles covered with brown scales or scurf; fruit a capsule ....Rhododendron lapponicum
            30. Twigs and petioles not covered with brown scales or scurf.
              31. Leaves glaucous on the lower surface.
                  Vaccinium (cranberries) p. 74
              31. Leaves green on the lower surface.
                32. Leaves with black dots on the lower surface, mostly 15–30 mm. long ....Vaccinium Vitis-Idaea
                32. Leaves without black dots on the lower surface, mostly 6–20 mm. long, obovate-spatulate.
                  Arctostaphylos Uva-ursi
        27. Stems erect.
        33. Stipule scars encircling the twig ....Magnolia p. 56
        33. Stipule scars not encircling the twig, (usually absent).
          34. Lower surface of leaves covered with dense woolly, rusty-brown hairs; fruit a capsule ....Ledum groenlandicum
          34. Lower surface of leaves not densely rusty-brown hairy.
            35. Stipules very small, black, spine-like, persistent; fruit a berry ....Ilex p. 54
            35. Stipules absent or not as above.
              36. Leaves mostly less than 5 cm. long; low shrubs; fruit a capsule.
                37. Leaves white on the lower surface, linear-lanceolate, revolute ....Andromeda glaucophylla
                37. Leaves pale green on the lower surface, broader, often many of them opposite or whorled.
                  38. Leaves subsessile, 6–13 mm. long.
                    Leiophyllum buxifolium

    38. Leaves with distinct petioles, mostly 2–6 cm. long . . .**Kalmia angustifolia**
  36. Leaves mostly 5–25 cm. long; tall shrubs or trees.
     39. Leaves clustered near the end of the season's growth; bark often reddish-
       brown, usually peeling off; fruit a 5-valved capsule.
       40. Leaves rugulose, whitish or rusty on lower surface; growth of pre-
         ceding season with numerous scale-scars below the leaves; capsule
         oblong . . . .**Rhododendron** p. 66
       40. Leaves not rugulose, light green on lower surface; growth of preceding
         season with two scale-scars at base; capsule subglobose. .**Kalmia** p. 55
     39. Leaves not clustered near the end of the season's growth; buds clustered
       on the end of twigs; fruit an acorn . . . .**Quercus** p. 63
26. Leaves deciduous.
    41. Leaves and young twigs covered with silvery or silvery and brown scales;
      thorns often present; fruit drupe-like . . . .**Elaeagnus** p. 51
    41. Leaves and twigs not covered with silvery scales.
     42. Leaves and bark spicy-aromatic.
       43. Leaves with three principal veins from near the base, often lobed;
         bark of branchlets green; drupe blue . . . .**Sassafras albidum** p. 82
       43. Leaves with one principal vein (midrib), never lobed; bark of branch-
         lets brown; drupe red . . . .**Lindera** p. 55
     42. Leaves and bark not spicy-aromatic.
       44. Leaves broadly cordate or oblique, with 3–7 large veins from the base.
         45. Stems climbing; vines; fruit a capsule . . . .**Aristolochia** p. 43
         45. Stems erect; trees or shrubs.
           45a. Leaf base cordate; fruit a legume . . . .**Cercis canadensis**
           45a. Leaf base oblique; fruit a drupe . . . .**Celtis laevigata**
       44. Leaves not cordate, or else with a midrib only.
         46. Vines or scrambling shrubs; fruit a red berry.
           47. Leaves ovate, base often cordate or lobed; crushed leaves and
             stems with strong, disagreeable odor . . . .**Solanum dulcamara**
           47. Leaves oblong or lanceolate with cuneate base; stems often with
             short thorn-like branches . . . .**Lycium halimifolium**
         46. Erect shrubs or trees.
           48. Twigs and leaves with milky sap; spines or thorns often present;
             fruit multiple . . . .**Maclura pomifera**
           48. Twigs and leaves without milky sap.
             49. Stems with branched or simple spines; inner bark and wood
               yellow; fruit red, berry-like . . . .**Berberis Thunbergii**
             49. Stems without spines; inner bark not yellow.
               50. Base of petioles hollow, covering the lateral buds; bark very
                 fibrous and leathery . . . .**Dirca palustris**
               50. Base of petioles not hollow; buds axillary.
                 50a. Bark very fibrous and leathery . . . .**Daphne Mezereum**
                 50a. Bark not decidedly leathery.

51. Lateral veins running parallel to the margins of the leaf and ending near the apex ....**Cornus alternifolia**
51. Lateral veins breaking up before reaching the margin of the leaf, not running to the apex.
  52. Pith divided by woody plates.
    53. Leaves 5–15 cm. in length; buds not silky ....**Nyssa sylvatica**
    53. Leaves 20–30 cm. long; buds dark, silky ....**Asimina triloba**
  52. Pith not divided by woody plates.
    54. Stipules and stipule-scars encircling the twig; leaves 10–30 cm. long, acuminate ....**Magnolia** p. 56
    54. Stipule scars absent or not encircling the twig; leaves smaller.
      55. Stipules small, black, spine-like; fruit a red berry ....**Ilex** p. 54
      55. Stipules not as above.
        56. Buds clustered at the end of twigs. (In the absence of buds in *Rhododendron* this condition may be ascertained by the falsely whorled arrangement of the twigs and leaves.)
          57. Leaves mostly clustered near the end of twigs, thin, margin ciliate; shrubs; fruit an elongated capsule on a glandular-pubescent pedicel ....**Rhododendron** p. 66
          57. Leaves scattered on the twigs, thick, margin not ciliate; trees; fruit an acorn ....**Quercus** p. 63
        56. Buds not clustered at the end of twigs.
          58. Each bud covered by a single hood-like scale ....**Salix** p. 70
          58. Each bud covered by two or more scales.
            59. Blades of leaves small, 1–10 cm. long.
              60. Petioles 1–4 cm. long.
                61. Apex of leaf often mucronate; fruit red, drupe-like.
                    Nemopanthus p. 85
                61. Apex of leaf obtuse or rounded.
                  61a. Leaves hairy below, apex obtuse; fruit a pome.
                    Cydonia oblonga
                  61a. Leaves glabrous, apex rounded; fruit red, drupe-like.
                    Cotinus Coggyria
              60. Petioles less than 1 cm. long or absent.
                62. Lower surface of leaves covered with yellow, resinous dots.
                  63. Leaves when crushed sweet-scented, often serrate near apex; fruit a waxy drupe ....**Myrica** p. 57
                  63. Leaves not sweet-scented.
                    64. Fruit a capsule ....**Lyonia mariana** p. 56
                    64. Fruit a berry ....**Gaylussacia** p. 52
                62. Lower surface of leaves not as above.
                  65. Branchlets greenish or reddish and minutely white-speckled or hairy, or the buds subglobose and spreading; fruit a berry ....**Vaccinium** p. 74
                  65. Branchlets not greenish or reddish or minutely white-speckled; fruit a capsule or drupe.

65a. Bark not shreddy; leaves with 6–7 pairs of lateral veins; fruit a drupe.
 Rhamnus p. 66

65a. Branchlets with gray or brownish shreddy bark; fruit globular or urn-shaped capsules in naked racemes .... **Lyonia** p. 56

59. Blades of leaves mostly larger, 8–20 cm. long.

66. Exposed bud-scales two; pith often chambered; bark breaking into regular blocks on older trunks; fruit a berry .... **Diospyros virginiana**

66. Exposed bud-scales several, imbricated; pith continuous; bark smooth, scaly, or ridged.

67. Leaf-blade more than twice as long as wide, tapering at both ends; fruit a drupe .... **Leitneria floridana**

67. Leaf-blade shorter, usually cordate or obtuse at base; fruit a pome.
 Pyrus p. 77

24. Margin of leaves not entire, (usually serrate, dentate, etc.).

68. Leaves with hard spines terminating the teeth; fruit a red berry. . **Ilex opaca**

68. Leaves without hard spines.

69. Plants with spines or thorns on stems, branches or twigs.

70. Twigs and branches armed with branched spines; inner bark and wood yellow; fruit red, berry-like .... **Berberis** p. 44

70. Twigs and branches armed with thorns.

71. Stipules reniform, large; fruit a pome . . **Chaenomeles lagenaria** p. 83

71. Stipules absent, or if present, not reniform.

72. Petioles with glands near the upper end; fruit a drupe. **Prunus** p. 61

72. Petioles without glands near the upper end; fruit a pome.

73. Thorns on twigs and branches; thorns without lateral buds; carpels stony .... **Crataegus** p. 83

73. Thorns on branches only; thorns usually leafy or with lateral buds; carpels not stony .... **Pyrus** p. 77

69. Plants without spines and thorns on stems and branches.

74. Stems climbing or twining; vines.

74a. Lateral veins of leaves straight and parallel; leaf margin serrulate; fruit a berry .... **Berchemia scandens**

74a. Lateral veins not straight; leaf margin crenate-serrate; fruit an orange capsule .... **Celastrus scandens**

74. Stems erect; shrubs or trees.

75. Stems low, 1–2 dm. high, almost herbaceous, from subterranean creeping stems; leaves persistent, glossy, coriaceous, clustered near the end of the season's growth.

76. Leaves oval, with wintergreen flavor; fruit red, berry-like.
 Gaultheria procumbens

76. Leaves oblanceolate or with main veins of lighter green, without wintergreen flavor; fruit a capsule .... **Chimaphila** p. 47

75. Stems more than 2 dm. high.

77. Leaves with 3–5 nearly equal main veins from near the base.

78. Low, weak, almost herbaceous, much branched shrubs; fruit a capsule.
Ceanothus p. 47

78. Trees or tall shrubs.
  79. Sap milky; fruit multiple and fleshy.
    80. Leaves glossy and smooth on upper surface; base of leaf oblique.
Morus alba p. 57

    80. Leaves rough or scabrous on upper surface.
      81. Base of leaf oblique, lower surface velvety...**Broussonetia papyrifera**
      81. Base of leaf not oblique, lower surface pubescent ..**Morus rubra** p. 57
  79. Sap not milky.
    82. Base of leaf not oblique; petiole usually flattened ....**Populus** p. 60
    82. Base of leaf oblique.
      83. Leaves long, taper-pointed; pith usually chambered; bark of trunk with high, corky ridges; fruit a drupe ....**Celtis** p. 47
      83. Leaves about as broad as long, cordate; pith not chambered; bark of trunk without corky ridges; fruit a small nut attached to a wing-like leaf ....**Tilia americana**

77. Leaves with one main vein (midrib) from the base.
  84. Buds distinctly stalked; leaves broad.
    85. Leaves crenate-dentate to wavy, base oblique; buds sickle-shaped and woolly; fruit a two-celled woody pod ....**Hamamelis virginiana**
    85. Leaves serrate or doubly-serrate to wavy, base not oblique; buds club-shaped, not woolly, often somewhat sticky; fruit small nutlets in persistent cone-like woody structure ....**Alnus** p. 42
  84. Buds not stalked, (except flower buds of *Chamaedaphne*).
    86. Base of leaf oblique; leaves two-ranked.
      86a. Leaves mostly doubly-serrate; serrations without glands; fruit a samara ....**Ulmus** p. 73
      86a. Leaves serrate; serrations gland-tipped; fruit a nut ......**Planera** p. 81
    86. Base of leaf not, or but slightly, oblique.
      87. Buds naked; fruit berry-like ....**Rhamnus** p. 66
      87. Buds scaly.
        88. Each bud covered by a single hood-like scale ....**Salix** p. 70
        88. Each bud covered by two or more scales.
          89. Leaves coarsely dentate or serrate, never doubly-serrate.
            90. Leaves short and broad.
              91. Petioles flattened or marginal teeth incurved; plant without thorns ....**Populus** p. 60
              91. Petioles not flattened; marginal teeth not incurved; plant often thorny ....**Crataegus** p. 83
            90. Leaves elongated; petioles not flattened.
              92. Terminal buds clustered; leaves oblong-lanceolate; trunk with rough bark; fruit an acorn ....**Quercus** p. 63
              92. Terminal buds not clustered; fruit a four-valved prickly bur.

93. Leaves oblong-ovate; buds long and sharp-pointed; terminal bud present; trunk with smooth, gray bark; bur with two triangular nuts.

Fagus grandifolia

93. Leaves oblong-lanceolate; buds ovate and blunt; terminal bud absent; trunk with rough furrowed bark; bur with 1–3 nuts .... **Castanea p. 47**

89. Leaves not coarsely serrate or dentate, mostly finely or doubly serrate, serrulate, denticulate or crenate, (sometimes entire near the base).

94. Branches green, ridged; leaves doubly serrate; (low shrub). **Kerria japonica**

94. Branches not green, or if green, then leaves not doubly serrate.

95. Pith chambered.

95a. Leaves with stellate pubescence on the lower surface; fruit dry, four-winged .... **Halesia carolina**

95a. Leaves without stellate pubescence; fruit a two-valved capsule.

Itea virginica

95. Pith continuous.

96. Base of leaf broad, cordate, truncate or nearly so; trees or tall shrubs.

97. Petioles with one or more glands near the upper end **Prunus p. 61**

97. Petioles without glands.

98. Leaf margin evenly and apparently simply serrate, dentate or crenate; leaves usually in more than two ranks.

99. Leaves broadly ovate or deltoid; petioles usually flattened.

Populus p. 60

99. Leaves not broadly ovate or deltoid; petioles never flattened.

100. Leaves 1–4 cm. long, not waxy on upper surface; fruit a berry-like pome .... **Amelanchier p. 43**

100. Leaves 5–8 cm. long, waxy on upper surface; fruit a pome.

Pyrus p. 77

98. Leaf margin unevenly and mostly doubly serrate or dentate; leaves mostly in two ranks.

101. Branches of mature trees with corky ridges **Ulmus Thomasii**

101. Branches of mature trees without corky ridges.

102. Branches with short spurs bearing 2 leaves or crowded leaf scars and terminated by a single bud; bark on younger trunks smooth or peeling off in rolls; lenticels elongated horizontally; twigs and inner bark often with wintergreen flavor; fruit a samara, in cone-like catkins **Betula p. 44**

102. Branches without short spurs; bark never peeling off in rolls; wintergreen flavor absent.

103. Leaves ovate or ovate-oblong, not taper-pointed, hairy; twigs mostly with bristly hairs; shrubs; fruit a nut within a husk-like involucre .... **Corylus p. 49**

103. Leaves much longer than broad, taper-pointed; leaves and twigs more or less glabrate.

104. Lateral veins unbranched; buds with flattened sides; bark smooth and sinewy-fluted; fruit a nutlet with bract-like appendage, several grouped in a flexuous spike ....**Carpinus caroliniana**

104. Lateral veins branched near margin of leaf; buds terete; bark rough, breaking off in scaly plates; fruit a nutlet enclosed in an inflated bag, several grouped in a cone-like spike ....**Ostrya virginiana**

96. Base of leaf acute or tapering.

105. Petioles with one or more glands at the upper end, or the lower surface of leaf waxy and with a dense row of light brown hairs along each side of mid-rib in *Prunus serotina;* fruit a drupe ....**Prunus p. 61**

105. Petioles without glands at the upper end; midrib of leaf without rows of hairs as above.

106. First bud-scale of lateral buds anterior; terminal bud long, sharp-pointed and resinous; leaves glabrous; fruit a capsule ....**Populus p. 60**

106. First bud-scale of lateral buds not anterior; terminal bud absent, or if present, mostly blunt.

107. Leaves with a sour taste, 1–1.5 dm. long, oblong-lanceolate, serrulate; fruit a five-valved capsule, numerous in panicled racemes.
Oxydendrum arboreum

107. Leaves without sour taste, less than 1 dm. long, or if longer, then not oblong-lanceolate; fruit various.

108. Midrib of leaf with dark glands on the upper surface; fruit a berry-like pome ....**Pyrus p. 77**

108. Midrib of leaf without dark glands on the upper surface.

109. Lower surface of leaves covered with yellow glands, scurf or dots.

110. Stems with longitudinal ridges; leaves and twigs scurfy; buds globular, resinous; fruit an achene with pappus.
Baccharis halimifolia

110. Stems without longitudinal ridges.

111. Leaves, when crushed, sweet-scented, often entire towards base, lower surface covered with yellow, resinous glands; fruit a waxy drupe or a winged nutlet ....**Myrica p. 57**

111. Leaves not sweet-scented.

112. Leaves coriaceous, persistent, lower surface covered with yellowish scurf; fruit a capsule in one-sided leafy raceme.
Chamaedaphne calyculata

112. Leaves not coriaceous, deciduous, lower surface covered with yellowish resin globules; fruit berry-like.
Gaylussacia p. 52

109. Lower surface of leaves not covered with yellow glands or dots.

113. Twigs stout, mostly 3–5 mm. in diameter when mature; branches often with stout spurs; trees or tall shrubs; fruit a pome ....**Pyrus** p. 77
113. Twigs slender.
  114. Fruit fleshy.
    115. Branchlets finely white-speckled or hairy, green or reddish; fruit a berry ....**Vaccinium** p. 74
    115. Branchlets not finely white-speckled or hairy, usually gray or brown.
      116. Leaves pale green or whitish on the lower surface; fruit a drupe.
          Prunus pumila p. 61
      116. Leaves bright green on the lower surface; fruit berry-like.
        117. Stipules small, sharp, persistent, nearly black ....**Ilex** p. 54
        117. Stipules not as above, ephemeral.
          118. Leaves deciduous; peduncles slender ....**Rhamnus** p. 66
          118. Leaves persistent; peduncles short ....**Gaylussacia brachycera**
  114. Fruit dry, a capsule or follicle.
    119. Twigs stellate-pubescent; leaves coarsely serrate; fruit a three-valved capsule ....**Clethra** p. 47
    119. Twigs not stellate-pubescent.
      120. Leaves serrate or doubly serrate; fruit follicular, in corymbs or panicles ....**Spiraea** p. 72
      120. Leaves serrulate; fruit a five-valved capsule.
        121. Capsules in spike-like racemes ....**Leucothoë** p. 55
        121. Capsules in open clusters ....**Lyonia** p. 56

V. PLANTS WITH ALTERNATE COMPOUND LEAVES

1. Leaves bi- or tri-pinnately compound.
   2. Margin of ovate leaflets entire; fruit a legume ....**Gymnocladus dioica**
   2. Margin of leaflets not entire.
      3. Base of petiole sheathing the twig; leaflets often lobed or irregularly serrate.
         4. Stem prickly; wood not yellow; fruit drupe-like ....**Aralia** p. 43
         4. Stem not prickly; wood yellow; fruit a follicle ....**Zanthorhiza apiifolia**
      3. Base of petiole not sheathing the twig; leaflets serrate or crenate; stout thorns usually present; fruit a legume ....**Gleditsia** p. 53
1. Leaves once compound.
   5. Leaflets three.
      6. Stipules present; (stems and petioles often prickly; leaflets often more than three).
         7. Stipules adnate to the petiole about half its length or more ...**Rosa** p. 84
         7. Stipules not adnate to the petiole ....**Rubus** p. 69
      6. Stipules absent.
         8. Petiole winged; branches green, provided with stout branched thorns.
            Citrus trifoliata
         8. Petiole not winged; thorns absent.
            9. Branches with prominent longitudinal ridges, green; leaves nearly sessile; fruit a legume ....**Cytisus scoparius**
            9. Branches not ridged, not green; leaves with prominent petiole.
               10. Lateral buds visible in the axils of leaves.
                  11. Lateral leaflets not symmetrical; stems often with aerial rootlets; fruit a whitish drupe ....**Rhus Toxicodendron** p. 25
                  11. Lateral leaflets symmetrical; stems without aerial rootlets; fruit a legume ....**Laburnum anagyroides**
               10. Lateral buds imbedded in the bark, not visible; lateral leaflets nearly symmetrical; stems without aerial rootlets.
                  12. Petioles 1–3 cm. long; margin of leaflets crenate; fruit a red drupe ....**Rhus aromatica**
                  12. Petioles 5–10 cm. long; margin of leaflets entire or crenulate; fruit a samara ....**Ptelea trifoliata**
   5. Leaflets more than three.
      13. Leaves palmately compound.
         14. Stems with spines or prickles.
            15. Stems biennial; fruit aggregate ....**Rubus** p. 69
            15. Stems perennial; fruit berry-like ......**Acanthopanax Sieboldianus**
         14. Stems without spines or prickles; a vine climbing by branched tendrils; fruit a berry ....**Parthenocissus** p. 58
      13. Leaves pinnately compound.

16. Lateral buds hidden (base of petiole hollow, forming a hood-like covering over the lateral buds or these imbedded under the base of the petiole).
  17. Leaflets small, 1–5 cm. long.
    18. Leaflets about 1 cm. long, silky; low shrub with shreddy bark.
                                          Potentilla fruticosa
    18. Leaflets 2–5 cm. long, elliptical, not silky; fruit a legume.
      19. Thorns, spines and prickles absent . . . .**Sophora japonica**
      19. Thorns, spines or prickles usually present.
        20. Margin of leaflets entire; twigs usually with stipular spines or prickles; pith pinkish-white . . . . **Robinia p. 69**
        20. Margin of leaflets somewhat serrate or crenate; twigs usually with simple or branched thorns; pith salmon-colored . . . . . **Gleditsia p. 53**
  17. Leaflets large, 5–10 cm. long, not elliptical.
    20a. Leaflets tipped with hard spines . . . .**Berberis Aquifolium**
    20a. Leaflets not tipped with hard spines.
      21. Leaflets alternate, oval or ovate, with distinct petioles; sap not milky; fruit a legume . . . .**Cladrastis lutea**
      21. Leaflets opposite, elongated, nearly sessile; sap milky; fruit a drupe.
                                                  Rhus p. 67
16. Lateral buds evident, not imbedded under or surrounded by base of the petiole.
  22. Leaflets tipped with hard spines; (leaves leathery; wood and inner bark yellow) . . . .**Berberis Aquifolium**
  22. Leaflets not tipped with spines.
    23. Spines or thorns present on the stems and often the midrib of leaves.
      24. Stipules absent; leaflets dotted with pellucid glands; wood yellow; fruit a capsule . . . . **Zanthoxylum p. 77**
      24. Stipules present; leaflets without pellucid glands; wood not yellow.
        25. Stipules adnate to the petiole half its length or more; margin of leaflets evenly serrate . . . . **Rosa p. 84**
        25. Stipules not adnate to the petiole; margin of leaflets usually unevenly coarsely toothed or often doubly serrate . . . . **Rubus p. 69**
    23. Spines, thorns and prickles absent.
      26. Margin of leaflets entire.
        27. Stems twining, vines . . . .**Wisteria sinensis**
        27. Stems erect, shrubs or trees.
          28. Leaflets subtended by stipels . . . .**Amorpha fruticosa**
          28. Leaflets not subtended by stipels.
            29. Leaflets 1–3 cm. long.
              30. Leaflets glabrous or nearly so, 4–6 pairs on a long rhachis, mostly 2 cm. long; tall shrubs . . . .**Caragana arborescens**
              30. Leaflets silky, about 1 cm. long, crowded on a short rhachis; low dense shrub . . . .**Potentilla fruticosa**

29. Leaflets 5 or more cm. long, glabrous; trees or tall shrubs.
  31. Pith chambered; fruit a large nut .... **Juglans regia**
  31. Pith solid; fruit a small whitish drupe .... **Rhus** p. 67
26. Margin of leaflets not entire.
  32. Leaflets with glands on the lower surface of the small basal lobes; (leaflets 11–41; crushed leaves with rank odor; twigs very stout); fruit a samara.
Ailanthus altissima
  32. Leaflets without glands; fruit not a samara.
    33. Base of petiole clasping the twig; wood yellow ....**Zanthorhiza apiifolia**
    33. Base of petiole not clasping the twig; wood not yellow.
      34. Stipules present (sometimes ephemeral but then buds are red); leaves not glandular-hairy.
        35. Leaves coarsely serrate; terminal bud present; trees or tall shrubs; fruit red, berry-like .... **Pyrus** p. 77
        35. Leaves doubly serrate; terminal bud absent; low suffrutescent shrubs; fruit a capsule .... **Sorbaria sorbifolia**
      34. Stipules absent; leaves often glandular-hairy; buds not red; fruit a nut.
        36. Pith chambered; husk of nut indehiscent .... **Juglans** p. 54
        36. Pith solid; husk of nut dehiscing into four valves ...... **Carya** p. 46

Note on Poison-ivy and Poison-oak

The white-fruited, trifoliate, dermatitis-producing species of *Rhus* are treated by some authors in a separate genus, *Toxicodendron*. The poison-ivy or poison-oak of the northeastern United States has been subdivided into two to thirty or more species by various authors. Fernald recognizes two species, *Rhus radicans* L., including several varieties and forms, the socalled common poison-ivy so abundant in northeastern North America, and *Rhus Toxicodendron* L., the so-called poison-oak of the Coastal Plain region, a smaller shrubby form with leaves lobed.

For a detailed discussion see Fernald, M. L., Rhodora 43:589–599. 1941.

VI. PLANTS WITH OPPOSITE OR WHORLED LEAF-SCARS

1. Stems climbing or twining; vines.
    2. Stems with six or more prominent longitudinal ridges, often nearly herbaceous; fruit a cluster of hairy achenes . . . .**Clematis** p. 47
    2. Stems without prominent longitudinal ridges; fruit not an achene.
        3. Bundle-scars in a closed or nearly closed ring; fruit a large fusiform capsule.
            4. Stems often with aerial rootlets at the nodes; tendrils absent.
                                                                Campsis radicans
            4. Stems without aerial rootlets; leaf tendrils sometimes persisting.
                                                                Bignonia capreolata
        3. Bundle-scars usually three, in a crescent-shaped line.
            5. Stems climbing by aerial rootlets; fruit a capsule . . . .**Decumaria barbara**
            5. Stems twining, without aerial rootlets; fruit a berry . . . . . .**Lonicera** p. 55
1. Stems erect; trees or shrubs.
    6. Buds and twigs densely peltate-scaly; shrubs . . . .**Shepherdia** p. 72
    6. Buds and twigs not peltate-scaly.
        7. Bundle-scars one, or seemingly one, (sometimes very numerous and almost confluent thus forming a transverse, lunate, or U-shaped line).
            8. Leaf-scars strongly decurrent or raised; fruit a capsule.
                9. Pith hollow or chambered; twigs olive-green or brownish; buds fusiform; bud-scales thin . . . .**Forsythia** p. 52
                9. Pith solid or only incompletely chambered.
                    10. Bud-scales fleshy; terminal bud usually absent; twigs gray to brown . . . .**Syringa vulgaris**
                    10. Bud-scales not fleshy; terminal bud present; twigs bright green or reddish, often with corky wings . . . .**Evonymus** p. 51
            8. Leaf-scars scarcely, or not at all, decurrent.
                11. Bud-scales very loose and open; buds never sunken in the bark; bark exfoliating; low shrubs; fruit a capsule.
                    12. Stems prostrate or flexible and spreading; twigs two-winged beneath the leaf-scars . . . .**Ascyrum** p. 44
                    12. Stems erect; twigs usually angled beneath the leaf-scars.
                                                                Hypericum p. 53
                11. Bud-scales mostly close and firm or else absent; buds in a few cases sunken in the bark.
                    13. Leaf-scars connected by a distinct raised stipular line.
                        14. Buds submerged in the bark; leaf-scars often whorled, not raised on bases of petioles; bundle-scars U-shaped; fruit a head of nutlets . . . .**Cephalanthus occidentalis**
                        14. Buds normally axillary; leaf-scars strictly opposite, raised on persistent bases of petioles; bundle-scars nearly circular; fruit a berry . . . .**Symphoricarpos** p. 73

13. Leaf-scars not connected by a distinct stipular line (an indistinct line present in some species of *Fraxinus*).

   15. Buds naked, or the smaller ones covered with a pair of nearly valvate scales; (buds often superposed; twigs usually scurfy).

                                                           Callicarpa americana

   15. Buds covered with several scales.

      16. Twigs bright green or reddish, often glaucous, usually four-angled; trees or shrubs ....**Evonymus** p. 51

      16. Twigs brown or rarely olive.

         17. Twigs, or some of them, tipped with a short spine; buds appressed, black, acute; short spur-like branches often present; fruit a dark berry ....**Rhamnus cathartica**

         17. Twigs never tipped with a spine; buds divaricate or very obtuse and pale.

            18. Twigs slender, less than 2 mm. in diameter; fruit a berry.

                                               Ligustrum p. 55

            18. Twigs stout, more than 2 mm. in diameter.

               19. Buds scurfy, brown or black; bundle-scars often almost separate and very numerous, forming a long U-shaped line; trees; fruit a samara ....**Fraxinus** p. 52

               19. Buds not scurfy, nearly or quite glabrous, paler; bundle-scars forming a straight or curved line; shrubs or small trees.

                  20. Bud-scales fleshy, green or reddish; twigs glabrous; fruit a capsule ....**Syringa vulgaris**

                  20. Bud-scales not fleshy, brown; twigs usually hirsute; fruit a drupe ....**Chionanthus virginica**

7. Bundle-scars several, separate.

   21. Bundle-scars in a closed, or nearly closed, ellipse. (*Staphylea* sometimes has as few as four bundle-scars, which however form an ellipse when connected by a line.)

      22. Stipule-scars present; ellipse of bundle-scars transverse; leaf-scars broadly crescent-shaped; older twigs finely white-striped.

                                             Staphylea trifolia

      22. Stipule-scars absent; ellipse longitudinal; leaf-scars orbicular. (*Broussonetia* sometimes has opposite leaf-scars. It has no terminal bud and its sap is milky. See page 32.)

         23. Pith chambered or hollow; ellipse of bundles not quite closed; leaf-scars opposite; fruit a short capsule ....**Paulownia tomentosa**

         23. Pith solid; ellipse closed; leaf-scars opposite or whorled; fruit a long capsule ....**Catalpa** p. 47

   21. Bundle-scars not in a closed ellipse, three or more quite distinct, in a lunate, U- or V-shaped line.

      24. Buds sunken in the bark or imbedded under the leaf-scars, (usually bursting through in late winter); shrubs.

25. Twigs spicy-aromatic; fruit falsely capsular ....**Calycanthus p. 45**
25. Twigs not spicy-aromatic.
  26. Buds imbedded under the leaf-scars; twigs unbranched **Philadelphus p. 58**
  26. Buds imbedded in the bark, superposed; twigs branched and striated.
        Iva frutescens
24. Buds axillary.
  27. Stems with hollow pith between the nodes; twigs gray or whitish; fruit a
     berry ....**Lonicera p. 55**
  27. Stems with solid pith.
    28. Bud-scales of axillary buds 0–3 pairs or solitary (sometimes 1–2 pairs of
      extra bracteoles beneath).
      29. Bud-scale one ....**Salix purpurea**
      29. Bud-scales 0–3 pairs.
        30. Buds without scales, densely tomentose, the foliage leaves serving as
          bud-scales; shrubs; fruit drupe-like.
          31. Buds small and slender ....**Rhamnus Frangula**
          31. Buds large and stout ....**Viburnum p. 74**
        30. Buds scaly, not tomentose, often silky.
          32. Buds scurfy, linear-lanceolate, often curved; fruit drupe-like.
             Viburnum p. 74
          32. Buds not scurfy, shorter.
            33. Junction of the upper leaf-scars forming a raised projection;
               bud-scales three pairs, often with buds in their axils; twigs
               olive or reddish, often glaucous or polished; fruit a samara.
                  Acer Negundo p. 41
            33. Junction of the leaf-scars not forming a raised projection, often
               notched instead; bud-scales 1–3 pairs.
              34. First pair of bud-scales shorter than the bud; shrubs; fruit a
                 drupe ....**Viburnum p. 74**
              34. First pair of bud-scales as long as the bud (until swelling
                 begins).
                35. Bud-scales, one pair; a pair of petiole bases persisting about
                   the terminal buds; shrubs or trees; fruit a drupe.
                      Cornus p. 48
                35. Bud-scales, two pairs (only one pair exposed); no per-
                   sistent petiole bases present.
                   36. Second pair of bud-scales hairy; twigs pubescent or
                     older bark white-striped; shrubs or trees; fruit a samara.
                        Acer p. 41
                  36. Second pair of bud-scales glabrous or glutinous; twigs
                     not pubescent; older bark not white-striped; shrubs;
                     fruit drupe-like ....**Viburnum p. 74**
    28. Bud-scales of axillary buds four to many pairs.

37. Bundle-scars normally five to many; leaf-scars broad; twigs stout.
  38. Terminal bud present; pith small; trees; fruit a capsule with large nut-like seeds ....**Aesculus** p. 42
  38. Terminal bud absent; pith very large; shrubs; fruit berry-like.
                                              Sambucus p. 72
37. Bundle-scars normally three, rarely five; leaf-scars narrow; twigs stout or slender.
  39. Decurrent hairy ridge from line connecting leaf-scars; shrubs; fruit a capsule ....**Diervilla Lonicera**
  39. Decurrent ridge from between leaf-scars absent.
    40. Leaf-scars ciliate; buds bronze-brown; terminal bud absent; shrubs; fruit a cluster of black nutlets ....**Rhodotypos kerrioides**
    40. Leaf-scars not ciliate, or if so, then terminal bud present.
      41. Bud-scales of previous year's buds persisting at the base of twigs; shrubs.
        42. Leaf-scars opposite; buds often superposed; fruit a berry.
                                  Lonicera p. 55
        42. Leaf-scars whorled or opposite; buds not superposed; fruit a capsule.
                                Hydrangea p. 53
      41. Bud-scales of previous year's buds not persisting.
        43. Upper edge of leaf-scar strongly concave; fruit a samara; trees.
                                  Acer p. 41
        43. Upper edge of leaf-scar nearly straight; inner bark yellow, very bitter; fruit a berry; shrubs or small trees ....**Rhamnus** p. 66

VII. PLANTS WITH ALTERNATE LEAF-SCARS

(The leaf-scars on short spurs may be clustered or appear whorled.)

1. Trees with fibrous bark; fruit a globular cone; gymnosperms. (Many of the twigs are deciduous and form scars which resemble leaf-scars.)
   Taxodium distichum
1. Trees, shrubs or vines; bark not fibrous.
   2. Leaf-scars, except on the young shoots, densely clustered on short spur-like branches; bark often resinous; trees; gymnosperms. (*Betula,* etc., in which each leaf-scar contains more than two bundle-scars belong in the next "2" below.)
      3. Bundle-scar one; twigs slender; fruit a cone ....**Larix p. 55**
      3. Bundle-scars two; twigs stout; fruit drupe-like ....**Ginkgo biloba**
   2. Leaf-scars mostly scattered along the twigs; angiosperms.
      4. Bundles in the stem scattered; stem brier-like, green, often prickly; petiole base persisting; climbing shrubs; fruit a berry; monocotyledons.
         Smilax p. 72
      4. Bundles in the stem in a ring; dicotyledons.
         5. Stems climbing or twining; vines.
            6. Tendrils present; fruit a berry.
               7. Woody partitions through the brownish pith usually present at the nodes; outer bark usually forming loose strips ....**Vitis p. 76**
               7. Woody partitions absent at the nodes; pith continuous; outer bark solid ....**Parthenocissus**
            6. Tendrils absent.
               8. Buds in slightly supra-axillary depressions; leaf-scars usually orbicular; twigs green.
                  8a. Twigs pubescent; drupe red ....**Cocculus p. 81**
                  8a. Twigs glabrous or nearly so.
                     8b. Stems slender, green, often suffrutescent; drupe less than 1 cm. in diameter, blue ....**Menispermum p. 81**
                     8b. Stems stouter; drupe at least 2 cm. long, black.
                        Calycocarpum p. 81
               8. Buds normal, axillary; leaf-scars variously shaped.
                  9. Stems prickly; leaf-scars very narrow; fruit berry-like **Rosa p. 84**
                  9. Stems not prickly (thorns often present in *Lycium*).
                     10. Bundle-scars 3–7, distinct; buds tomentose.
                        11. Twigs green, twining; buds clustered; fruit a capsule.
                           Aristolochia p. 43
                        11. Twigs not green, climbing by rootlets; buds solitary; (juice resinous); fruit a whitish drupe; *poisonous.*
                           Rhus Toxicodendron
                     10. Bundle-scars one, or several confluent scars appearing as one.
                        12. Pith hollow; stem often almost herbaceous, green or whitish, with a strong odor; twigs angled; leaf-scars raised; fruit a red berry ....**Solanum dulcamara**

12. Pith solid or chambered; odor not strong.
  13. Buds silky; (leaf-scars often 2-horned on the lower side, projecting, not decurrent); fruit a legume .... **Wisteria sinensis**
  13. Buds glabrous or nearly so.
    14. Stems ridged, often thorny; buds blunt, often clustered; fruit a red berry .... **Lycium halimifolium**
    14. Stems not ridged, not thorny; buds solitary.
      14a. Buds divaricate; leaf-scars not raised; fruit an orange capsule with red pulp around the seeds .... **Celastrus scandens**
      14a. Buds appressed; leaf-scars raised; fruit a black berry.
        Berchemia scandens
5. Stems not climbing or twining; mostly erect trees or shrubs, rarely prostrate.
  15. Bundle-scars more than one. (For other "15" see p. 38.)
    16. Bundle-scars more than three, in any arrangement except a single lunate line.
      17. Thorns usually present beside flat-topped, depressed buds; branches light olive-gray; fruit multiple, large and fleshy .... **Maclura pomifera**
      17. Thorns absent; buds neither flat-topped nor depressed.
        18. Stipule-scars or stipules present.
          19. Terminal bud present.
            20. Stipule-scars extending less than half way around the twig.
              21. Buds depressed, indistinct, white-tomentose with branched hairs; scales irregular; shrubs or small trees; fruit a capsule.
                Hibiscus syriacus
              21. Buds ovate, prominent, not tomentose, clustered near the end of twigs; twigs often angled or fluted; trees or large shrubs; fruit an acorn .... **Quercus p. 63**
            20. Stipule-scars extending nearly or completely around the twig.
              22. Bud-scales several, imbricated.
                23. Buds brown, lanceolate; bundle-scars not in a ring; sap watery .... **Fagus grandifolia**
                23. Buds green, not lanceolate; bundle-scars in a ring; sap milky .... **Ficus carica**
              22. Bud-scales one or two, united into a cap; (fruit aggregate, resembling a cone).
                24. Bud-scales one, with a scar on the back; leaf-scars mostly lunate; fruit a fleshy "cone" .... **Magnolia p. 56**
                24. Bud-scales two, valvate; leaf-scars mostly orbicular; fruit a "cone", at least its axis persisting.
                Liriodendron tulipifera
          19. Terminal bud absent.
            25. Visible bud-scales four or more or catkins present.
              26. Buds deltoid, appressed or slightly spreading; trees; fruit multiple, berry-like .... **Morus p. 57**

26. Buds oval, spreading; tall shrubs; fruit a nut with an involucre.
Corylus p. 49

  25. Visible bud-scales two or three; catkins wanting in winter; trees.

    27. Twigs scabrous, often mottled; sap milky; fruit multiple, berry-like.
Broussonetia papyrifera

    27. Twigs glabrous or puberulent.

      28. Buds and twigs reddish or olive, twigs usually zigzag; pith terete; fruit drupe-like, attached to a leafy bract . . . . .Tilia p. 86

      28. Buds and twigs light olive-brown; twigs nearly straight; pith five-sided; fruit a nut with prickly involucre . . . . .Castanea p. 47

18. Stipule-scars and stipules absent.

  29. Leaf-scars nearly circular; twigs slender; axillary buds not visible; flower buds terminal, like young catkins; low or decumbent shrubs with strong odor; fruit a drupe . . . . .Rhus aromatica

  29. Leaf-scars inversely triangular or oblong; twigs stout.

    30. Bark of twigs mottled; juice resinous; lateral buds small, solitary; *poisonous* shrubs; fruit a whitish drupe . . . . .Rhus p. 67

    30. Bark of twigs not mottled; juice not resinous; lateral buds large, super-posed; trees; fruit a nut . . . . .Carya p. 46

16. Bundle-scars three or more in a single lunate line. (In *Juglans* sometimes three U-shaped groups which form a lunate line. If the leaves are not deciduous at the base then the bundle-scars must be counted in a section cut through the base of the petiole.)

  31. Stipule-scars or stipules present.

    31a. Branches thorny . . . . .Chaenomeles lagenaria

    31a. Branches not thorny.

      32. Terminal bud present.

        33. Buds stalked.

          34. Buds densely tomentose; pith terete; fruit a woody capsule.
Hamamelis virginiana

          34. Buds scurfy or glutinous; pith 3-sided; fruit cone-like . .Alnus p. 42

        33. Buds sessile.

          34a. Buds naked . . . . .Rhamnus p. 66

          34a. Buds scaly.

            35. First scale of axillary bud anterior; trees . . . . .Populus p. 60

            35. First scale of axillary bud lateral.

              36. Twigs brier-like, often prickly; stems biennial; leaves decidu-ous above the base; fruit aggregate . . . . .Rubus p. 69

              36. Twigs not brier-like, never prickly.

                37. Leaf-scars strongly decurrent; bark light brown, shreddy; fruit follicular . . . . .Physocarpus opulifolius

                37. Leaf-scars slightly or not at all decurrent.

                  38. Buds silky; (bark green and firm, with odor of fresh bean pods); fruit a legume . . . . .Laburnum anagyroides

                  38. Buds not silky.

                    39. Last season's growth branched.

40. Low weak shrubs; fruit of three small nutlets; fruit bases usually persistent ....Ceanothus p. 47
40. Tall shrubs or small trees; twigs often hairy; fruit a hairy pome.
    Cydonia oblonga
39. Last season's growth unbranched; trees or tall shrubs.
    41. Stipule-scars lateral to the leaf-scars; visible bud-scales usually three; twigs often with wintergreen flavor; fruit cone-like ....Betula p. 44
    41. Stipule-scars slightly above or behind the leaf-scars; visible bud-scales more than three; flavor, if any, like that of bitter almonds; fruit a drupe.
        Prunus p. 61
32. Terminal bud absent.
    42. Stipule-scars extending entirely around the stem; leaf-scar nearly encircling the bud; bud with one scale; trees; fruit a stalked globular head of hairy achenes. ....Platanus p. 60
    42. Stipule-scars not extending around the stem.
        42a. Buds naked ....Rhamnus p. 66
        42a. Buds with one or more scales.
            43. Bud-scale one, hood-like, the suture down the inner face of the bud.
                Salix p. 70
            43. Bud-scales more than one.
                44. Exposed bud-scales two or three (rarely four).
                    45. Twigs coarsely striate; buds superposed; shrubs; fruit a legume.
                        Amorpha fruticosa
                    45. Twigs not striate; buds not superposed; trees.
                        46. Buds globular-ovate; twigs zigzag; fruit drupe-like, dry, attached to a leafy bract ....Tilia americana
                        46. Buds elongated-acute; twigs not zigzag; often with wintergreen flavor; spurs with a terminal bud; fruit cone-like ...Betula p. 44
                44. Exposed bud-scales four to many.
                    47. Leaf-scars in two ranks.
                        48. Bud-tips appressed, brown; pith mostly chambered; trees; fruit a drupe ....Celtis p. 47
                        48. Bud-tips not appressed; pith not chambered.
                            49. Bud-scales evidently in two vertical rows; bundle-scars typically sunken in a smooth, corky layer which covers the leaf-scars; bark ridged; catkins and spurs absent.
                                49a. Buds ovoid; twigs not dark red ....Ulmus p. 73
                                49a. Buds globose or short conical; twigs dark red .Planera p. 81
                            49. Bud-scales not in two rows; bundle-scars not sunken in a corky layer; fruit borne in catkins.
                                50. Last season's growth densely covered at base with leaf-scars, numerous short spurs on older wood with many leaf-scars and a terminal bud; bark often wintergreen-flavored; lenticels elongated; staminate catkins usually present in winter ....Betula p. 44
                                50. Last season's growth not as above; no such spurs or flavor.

51. Buds usually 3–7 mm. long, terete; bud-scales often striate; bark of trunk scaly, dark gray; staminate catkins usually present in winter.
Ostrya virginiana

51. Buds usually 2–4 mm. long, often four-sided; bud-scales four-ranked, not striate; bark smooth, sinewy-fluted, light gray; staminate catkins not present in winter ....**Carpinus caroliniana**

47. Leaf-scars not in two ranks.

  52. Brier-like shrubs, often prickly; stems biennial; leaves deciduous above the base; fruit aggregate, berry-like ....**Rubus** p. 69

  52. Plants not brier-like, never prickly; stems perennial; leaves not deciduous above the base.

    53. Bark of whole plant bright green; (a finely branched low shrub); fruit like an achene ....**Kerria japonica**

    53. Bark not bright green.

      54. Buds globular; twigs glandular, hairy, resinous, aromatic; staminate catkins near tip of twigs; fruit small, nut-like .....**Myrica peregrina**

      54. Buds ovate: twigs not glandular.

        55. Bud-scales dark brown or black; twigs gray or green; fruit berry-like ....**Rhamnus** p. 66

        55. Bud-scales red, gray, or light brown; twigs olive or red-brown.

          56. Stipule-scars lateral to the leaf-scars; fruit a pome.
Cydonia oblonga

          56. Stipule-scars above or behind the leaf-scars; fruit a drupe.
Prunus (*Plums*) p. 61

31. Stipule-scars and stipules absent, (except rarely as modified into spines).

  57. Terminal bud present.

    58. Pith chambered or with woody partitions.

      59. Pith chambered.

        60. Leaf-scars almost encircling the twigs; buds not superposed; bud-scales thin; low shrubs; fruit a follicle ....**Zanthorhiza apiifolia**

        60. Leaf-scars not encircling the twigs; buds superposed.

          60a. Buds large, at least 5 mm. long, with thick scales; fruit a nut; trees ....**Juglans** p. 54

          60a. Buds small, with thin scales; fruit a two-valved capsule; shrubs.
Itea virginica

      59. Pith with transverse woody partitions.

        61. Bundle-scars 5–7; lateral buds globular, densely dark-velvety; terminal bud naked; fruit large, berry-like ....**Asimina triloba**

        61. Bundle-scars three; lateral buds ovate, nearly or quite glabrous; terminal bud scaly; fruit a small drupe ....**Nyssa sylvatica**

    58. Pith continuous and homogenous.

      62. Bundle-scars more than three.

        63. Stems prickly, often very stout; fruit drupe-like.

64. Leaf-scars extending nearly around the twigs; bundle-scars about 20.
                      Aralia p. 43

64. Leaf-scars not extending more than half way around the stem; bundle-scars 5–10 ....**Acanthopanax Sieboldianus**

63. Stems not prickly.

 65. Leaf-scars extending nearly around the twigs; (wood bright yellow); low shrubs; fruit a follicle ....**Zanthorhiza apiifolia**

 65. Leaf-scars not extending more than half way around the twigs.

  66. Buds usually yellow or brownish; bark with resinous juice; fruit a white drupe; *poisonous* shrubs or vines ....**Rhus** p. 67

  66. Buds dark red, smooth or hairy; bark without resinous juice; base of petiole often persistent; fruit berry-like, red ....**Pyrus** p. 77

62. Bundle-scars three.

 67. Leaf-scar a narrow line extending about half way around the stem, not decurrent; plant often brier-like and prickly; fruit reddish, berry-like.
                      Rosa p. 84

 67. Leaf-scar broad or narrow, but not forming a line, usually decurrent.

  68. Twigs prickly or buds red-tomentose.

   69. Leaves deciduous above the base; recurved, brier-like shrubs.
                     Rubus p. 69

   69. Leaves deciduous at the base; twigs not conspicuously brier-like.

    70. Prickles one to three below each leaf-scar, the latter decurrent; twigs pale; buds lanceolate, with thin scales ....**Ribes** p. 68

    70. Prickles two at each leaf-scar or scattered; buds depressed, red-tomentose or nearly black ....**Zanthoxylum** p. 77

  68. Twigs not prickly, sometimes thorny; buds not red-tomentose.

   71. Leaf-scars semicircular or broadly lunate, large; trees or shrubs.

    72. Bark with resinous juice; (buds acute; fruit a drupe on plumose pedicel) ....**Cotinus Coggyria**

    72. Bark without resinous juice.

     73. First bud-scale of lateral buds anterior; bud-scales puberulent all over ....**Populus** p. 60

     73. First bud-scale of lateral buds not anterior.

      74. Bud-scales persisting at base of twigs; lenticels raised, circular; wood very light and soft; fruit a drupe. .....**Leitneria floridana**

      74. Bud-scales not persisting at base of twigs.

       75. Bud-scales ciliate, polished; broken buds resinous, aromatic; leaf-scars raised; branches often with corky winged ridges of bark; pith large, angular; fruit a head of many capsules.
                   Liquidambar styraciflua

       75. Bud-scales not ciliate; leaf-scars not prominently raised; corky ridges on bark absent; pith not angular; buds sometimes clustered; fruit a drupe ....**Prunus** p. 61

   71. Leaf-scars narrowly lunate, or small, 2 mm. or less in diameter.

76. Internodes very unequal, branches much exceeding the central axis; fruit a drupe ....**Cornus alternifolia**

76. Internodes not very unequal, branches shorter than the central axis.

  77. Buds superposed; collateral globose flower buds usually present; bark spicy-aromatic; shrubs; fruit red, drupe-like ....**Lindera p. 55**

  77. Buds not superposed; bark not spicy-aromatic.

    78. Buds much elongated, often pointed; thorns absent.

      79. Bark, at least the older, shreddy; leaf-scars often strongly decurrent; bud-scales very thin, often glandular; shrubs; fruit a berry.

                                                           Ribes p. 68

      79. Bark close, not shreddy; leaf-scars not decurrent; fruit a berry-like pome.

        80. Second bud-scale about half the length of bud or more, bud-scales glandular-toothed, rather thick, reddish; shrubs ......**Pyrus p. 77**

        80. Second bud-scale usually less than half the length of bud, bud-scales thin and closely appressed, mostly with a black tip; shrubs or trees ....**Amelanchier p. 43**

    78. Buds ovate, globular or depressed; branches often thorny; (buds narrowly ovate and lateral twigs thorn-like in *Pyrus coronaria*).

      81. Branchlets clustered near the end of each season's growth, often with minute golden resin-granules, at least above; scales of the terminal bud acute, the others rounded; shrubs; fruit a small waxy drupe or dry ....**Myrica p. 57**

      81. Branchlets more evenly distributed and without resin-granules; scales of terminal and lateral buds similar.

        82. Leaves deciduous above the base of petiole ....**Rubus p. 69**

        82. Leaves deciduous at the base of petiole.

          83. Plant a low or creeping shrub ....**Ribes p. 68**

          83. Plant a tree or tall shrub.

            84. Scales of terminal bud narrowly ovate, thick, reddish, mostly three-dentate; buds narrowly ovate; twigs dark red or bronze-gray; lateral twigs mostly sharp and thorn-like; small trees; fruit a pome ....**Pyrus p. 77**

            84. Scales of terminal bud broadly ovate, thinner and appressed; buds usually broadly ovate.

              85. Axillary buds flattened and closely appressed, broadly ovate, mostly hairy; twigs mostly dark, rarely olive; trees with a broad, spreading crown; fruit a pome with papery carpel walls ....**Pyrus p. 77**

              85. Axillary buds plump and divaricate, often sharp-pointed (sometimes appressed in *Pyrus*).

                85a. Buds obtuse, almost spherical, rarely acute; leaf-scars narrow; twigs and branches mostly with thorns; trees or shrubs; fruit a pome with stony carpel walls.

                                             Crataegus p. 83

85a. Buds acute, mostly glabrous, conical, sharp pointed; twigs mostly without thorns; trees with a narrow crown; fruit a pome ....**Pyrus communis**
57. Terminal bud absent.
 86. Bundle-scars five to many.
  87. Twigs spiny or bristly; stout; leaf-scars extending nearly around the stem; odor strong; fruit a berry ....**Aralia** p. 43
  87. Twigs not spiny or bristly; leaf-scar not extending half way around the stem.
   88. Leaf-scar extending nearly around the bud, deeply V-shaped; buds tomentose or silky.
    89. Bundle-scars projecting out of the almost white leaf-scar; buds brownish, superposed; wood yellow; fruit a legume..**Cladrastis lutea**
    89. Bundle-scars not projecting out of the leaf-scars; buds not superposed.
     90. Twigs very stout; bark with resinous juice; fruit a red drupe. **Rhus** p. 67
     90. Twigs slender; bark not resinous, very tough and fibrous; fruit a drupe ....**Dirca palustris**
   88. Leaf-scar semicircular, deltoid or lunate, extending not more than half way around the depressed bud; twigs very stout.
    91. Buds superposed, imbedded in the bark; pith salmon-colored; twigs with whitened epidermis; fruit a legume ......**Gymnocladus dioica**
    91. Buds solitary, exposed; pith ochraceous; twigs usually yellow-brown; fruit a samara ....**Ailanthus altissima**
 86. Bundle-scars three.
  92. Leaf-scars deeply V-shaped, partly surrounding the bud, or buds bursting through the leaf-scars.
   93. Buds in the upper angle of V-shaped leaf-scars, whitish, hairy, round, mostly superposed; twigs unarmed; fruit a samara ....**Ptelea trifoliata**
   93. Buds bursting through the leaf-scars; twigs usually armed with thorns, spines or prickles; fruit a legume.
    94. Buds distant, superposed, glabrous; stout branched thorns often present; twigs often nodose; pith of branchlets salmon-colored. **Gleditsia** p. 53
    94. Buds if superposed, contiguous, hairy; unbranched nodal spines or prickles usually present; twigs often strongly angled; pith pinkish-white ....**Robinia** p. 69
  92. Leaf-scars not deeply V-shaped, free from the buds.
   95. Leaf-scar very narrow, like a line extending half way around the stem; stems brier-like ....**Rosa** p. 84
   95. Leaf-scar broader, not extending half way around the stem.
    96. Buds mostly superposed.
     97. Twigs furrowed, green or gray-brown; fruit a head of hairy achenes ....**Baccharis halimifolі̇**

97. Twigs not furrowed, finely white-speckled.
   98. Twigs spicy-aromatic; globose collateral flower-buds often present; fruit a red drupe ....**Lindera** p. 55
   98. Twigs not spicy-aromatic; fruit a legume ....**Cercis canadensis**
96. Buds not superposed.
   99. Bark bright green; finely branched low shrubs ....**Kerria japonica**
   99. Bark not bright green.
      100. Bark resinous; leaf-scars semicircular; fruit a drupe ....**Rhus** p. 67
      100. Bark not resinous; leaf-scars lunate to nearly semicircular.
         101. Leaves deciduous 3–4 mm. above the base.
            102. Bud-scales blunt, terminated by a scar; foliar prickles usually present; inner bark yellow; shrubs; fruit a red berry.**Berberis** p. 44
            102. Bud-scales neither blunt nor terminated by a scar; prickles if present not foliar; inner bark not yellow; shrubs; fruit aggregate, berry-like ....**Rubus** p. 69
         101. Leaves deciduous at the base; prickles absent.
            103. Twigs polished, mostly zigzag; buds depressed, mostly obtuse; fruit a pome ....**Crataegus** p. 83
            103. Twigs not polished.
               104. Twigs brown or nearly black, often glandular, slender, with short internodes; fruit a drupelet ....**Myrica** p. 57
               104. Twigs pale brown, not glandular, stout, with long internodes; fruit several follicles ....**Sorbaria sorbifolia**
15. Bundle-scar one (sometimes spread out into a transverse line).
  105. Twigs peltate-scaly or stellate-pubescent.
     106. Young twigs stellate-pubescent; fruit a capsule ....**Clethra** p. 47
     106. Young twigs peltate-scaly; fruit a drupe ....**Elaeagnus** p. 51
  105. Twigs not peltate-scaly nor stellate-pubescent.
     107. Stipules or stipule-scars present; shrubs.
        108. Stipules persistent, (often very small).
           109. Stipules sheathing the stem; bark brown, shreddy; fruit long, hairy achenes ....**Potentilla fruticosa**
           109. Stipules not sheathing the stem, very minute.
              110. Twigs bright green, ridged, angled, or winged, wand-like, usually dying at the tip; fruit a legume ....**Cytisus scoparius**
              110. Twigs gray-brown or ashy.
                 111. Leaf-scars raised on persistent petiole base, decumbent; fruit a legume ....**Caragana arborescens**
                 111. Leaf-scars not raised; fruit a red or black berry ....**Ilex** p. 54

108. Stipules deciduous.
    112. Buds superposed; twigs often striate with gray and green or brown stripes; fruit a legume ....**Amorpha fruticosa**
    112. Buds not superposed.
        113. Low, weak, unarmed shrubs, dying nearly to the ground each winter; fruit of 3 small nutlets, the bases usually persisting ...**Ceanothus p. 47**
        113. Large shrubs or trees, usually with thorny branches; buds depressed, lateral to the thorns; fruit multiple, forming a large ball. (Compare also with *Celtis* in which bundle-scars are fused into one.)
                                                    Maclura pomifera
107. Stipule-scars or stipules absent.
    114. Terminal bud present.
        115. Bark spicy-aromatic; twigs green, branching freely the first season; branches surpassing the main axis; trees; fruit a blue drupe.
                                                    Sassafras albidum
        115. Bark not spicy-aromatic; shrubs.
            116. Leaf-scars even with surface of epidermis.
                117. Buds, except on strong shoots, clustered at the end of twigs; terminal bud often very large; lateral buds solitary, axillary; twigs not speckled; fruit a capsule ....**Rhododendron p. 66**
                117. Buds not clustered; lateral buds often superposed.
                    118. Twigs speckled; fruit a red drupe ....**Daphne Mezereum**
                    118. Twigs not speckled; fruit dry, four-winged ....**Halesia carolina**
            116. Leaf-scars, at least the upper edge, projecting slightly.
                119. Leaf-scars very rough and uneven; bark usually bronze-brown, tending to exfoliate; stems wand-like or much branched and recurved with slender twigs; fruit follicular ....**Spiraea p. 72**
                119. Leaf-scars scarcely uneven; bark on older branches gray, smooth, often with a white exfoliating crust; tall, much branched shrubs; stems neither wand-like nor recurved; fruit dark red, berry-like.
                                              Nemopanthus mucronata
114. Terminal bud absent.
    120. Branches with an axillary thorn at each node; buds lateral to the thorns; bark bright green, finely punctate with oil glands, fragrant; trees; fruit a berry ....**Citrus trifoliata**
    120. Branches and bark not as above.
        121. Twigs finely white-speckled or granulose, green or reddish; shrubs; fruit a berry ....**Vaccinium p. 74**
        121. Twigs neither white-speckled nor granulose.
            122. Trees.
                123. Pith chambered.
                    124. Buds superposed; fruit dry, four-winged ......**Halesia carolina**

124. Buds solitary, with two visible scales; fruit a large berry.

Diospyros virginiana

123. Pith continuous.

125. Visible bud-scales 4–6; fruit a five-celled capsule borne in spreading racemes ....**Oxydendrum arboreum**

125. Visible bud-scales 2 ....**Diospyros virginiana**

122. Shrubs.

126. Winter twigs often with reddish, catkinlike racemes of flowerbuds.

Leucothoë p. 55

126. Winter twigs not as above.

127. Twigs with two kinds of buds, the larger flower-buds with several visible scales, the shorter buds with two visible scales, all reddish-yellow, divaricate; twigs reddish, mostly pubescent; fruit a berry.

Gaylussacia p. 52

127. Twigs with only one kind of bud.

128. Visible bud-scales mostly two or three ....**Lyonia p. 56**

128. Visible bud-scales several.

129. Leaf-scars raised; fruit follicular ....**Spiraea p. 72**

129. Leaf-scars not raised; fruit a green berry ....**Vaccinium stamineum**

B. KEYS TO SPECIES

Abies—*Firs*

1. Leaves dark green and glossy above, pale below, 2–3 cm. long . . . . **A. balsamea**
1. Leaves pale blue-green, 5–8 cm. long . . . . **A. concolor**

Acer—*Maples*
Summer Key

1. Leaves pinnately compound . . . . **A. Negundo**
1. Leaves simple, mostly palmately lobed.
    2. Leaves silvery-white on lower surface.
        3. Lobes of leaves crenate-serrate; collateral buds absent . . **A. pseudoplatanus**
        3. Lobes of leaves remotely or sharply serrate.
            4. Buds pointed, not reddish; collateral buds absent . . . . . . **A. saccharum**
            4. Buds blunt, mostly reddish; collateral buds often present.
                5. Sinus V-shaped; branchlets straight . . . . **A. rubrum**
                5. Sinus U-shaped; branchlets arching upward . . . . **A. saccharinum**
    2. Leaves not silvery-white on lower surface.
        6. Lobes of leaves obtuse or rounded, with entire margin . . . . **A. campestre**
        6. Lobes of leaves acute or acuminate or leaves with serrate margin.
            7. Leaves unlobed, margin serrate . . . . **A. tataricum**
            7. Leaves lobed.
                8. Leaves mostly with three lobes, with serrate margins.
                    9. Buds with several pairs of imbricated scales, sessile . . . . **A. ginnala**
                    9. Buds with one pair of valvate scales visible, stalked.
                        10. Twigs and buds glabrous; bark of older branches white-striped.
                            A. pennsylvanicum
                        10. Twigs and buds pubescent; bark not striped . . . . . **A. spicatum**
                8. Leaves mostly with five lobes, with entire or coarsely dentate margins; buds sessile, with several pairs of imbricated scales.
                    11. Sap from broken petioles milky; buds green or red, stout and blunt . . . . **A. platanoides**
                    11. Sap from broken petioles not milky; buds brown, slender and acute.
                        12. Leaves pale green, glabrous or rarely pubescent below; stipules absent . . . . **A. saccharum**
                        12. Leaves yellow-green and pubescent below; stipules often present . . . . **A. nigrum**

Winter Key

1. Buds with two exposed valvate scales, strictly stalked; shrubs or small trees.
    2. Twigs and buds glabrous; bark white-striped . . . . **A. pennsylvanicum**
    2. Twigs and buds pubescent; bark not striped . . . . **A. spicatum**
1. Buds with several exposed scales, essentially sessile; mostly trees.
    3. Buds white-downy; twigs generally with a bloom; opposite leaf-scars meeting in a sharp-pointed raised projection . . . . **A. Negundo**
    3. Buds not white-downy; twigs without a bloom; opposite leaf-scars not meeting in a sharp-pointed raised projection.

4. Buds slender, sharp-pointed, with 4–8 pairs of visible brownish scales.
    5. Twigs slender, reddish-brown, glossy .... **A. saccharum**
    5. Twigs stout, orange-brown, dull, often mottled with gray ....**A. nigrum**
4. Buds stout, blunt, with fewer pairs of visible scales.
    6. Collateral buds often present; bud-scales reddish; terminal bud usually less than 5 mm. long; (leaf-scars usually not meeting).
        7. Bark flaking on old trunk, leaving brown areas; twigs with rank odor when broken ....**A. saccharinum**
        7. Bark of trunk rough but generally not flaking; twigs without rank odor when broken ....**A. rubrum**
    6. Collateral buds absent; bud-scales not red, except in *A. platanoides,* then terminal bud over 5 mm. long.
        8. Terminal bud large, over 5 mm. long; twigs stout.
            9. Buds red, appressed; edges of leaf-scars meeting ......**A. platanoides**
            9. Buds green, spreading; edges of leaf-scars not meeting.
                A. pseudoplatanus
        8. Terminal bud small, less than 5 mm. long, or absent; opposite leaf-scars joined by a line; twigs slender or medium; small trees or shrubs.
          10. Buds gray, hairy; twigs mostly pubescent; branchlets often corky.
                A. campestre
          10. Buds brown, glabrous; twigs glabrous..**A. tataricum** and **A. ginnala**

Aesculus—*Horse-chestnuts and Buckeyes*

1. Buds gummy; leaflets usually seven; fruit prickly ....**A. Hippocastanum**
1. Buds not gummy; leaflets usually five, acuminate.
    2. Buds elongated, mucronate; injured twigs with a strongly fetid odor; branchlets usually glossy; fruit prickly, at least when young ......**A. glabra**
    2. Buds ovate, acute; injured twigs with but a slightly fetid odor; branchlets usually dull; fruit not prickly ....**A. octandra**

Alnus—*Alders*

1. Buds sessile, reddish-purple, glutinous; leaves sharply serrulate, green on both surfaces; fertile catkins clustered on slender stalks; nutlets strongly winged; shrubs or small trees.
    2. Leaves, twigs and peduncles glabrous or nearly so ....**A. crispa**
    2. Leaves, twigs and peduncles pubescent ....**A. crispa** var. **mollis**
1. Buds stalked, scurfy; nutlets wingless or nearly so.
    3. Leaves with wedge-shaped base, pointed apex and sharply serrate margin; fertile catkins usually solitary; tree ....**A. maritima**
    3. Leaves with acute, obtuse, cordate or rounded base; fertile catkins clustered.
        4. Leaves obovate to orbicular, with notched or truncate apex and dentate or serrate margin; lateral buds with one or more scars on the stalk; tree.
                A. glutinosa

4. Leaves elliptical, ovate or obovate, neither notched nor truncate at apex; shrubs or small trees.
  5. Leaves obovate, base acute, margin finely serrate; staminate catkins nearly at right angles to the pistillate catkins; nutlets ovate . . **A. serrulata**
  5. Leaves broadly elliptical to ovate, base broad and rounded, margin doubly or coarsely serrate; staminate and pistillate catkins both drooping; nutlets orbicular . . . .**A. incana**

Amelanchier—*Juneberry, Shad Bush, Service Berry*

In general the characters used in this key will hold, especially if typical specimens are used. However, in some species, there are certain intermediate forms which may give difficulty. This key is based upon the characters used by Professor K. M. Wiegand in his treatment of the species of *Amelanchier* of the northeastern United States (See Rhodora *14*:117–161, 1912; 22:146–151, 1920.)

1. Petioles stout, 2–10 mm. long; leaves imbricated in the bud; leaf-base acute; flowers solitary (1–3 in a cluster) . . . .**A. Bartramiana**
1. Petioles slender, 8–25 mm. long; leaves conduplicate in the bud; flowers in racemes.
  2. Teeth of the leaves coarse (3–6 per cm.); veins conspicuous, usually straight, parallel and close together, short intermediate ones few or none.
    3. Leaves oval-oblong; upright, low, somewhat stoloniferous shrubs, about .5–1 meter high . . . .**A. humilis**
    3. Leaves oval-orbicular; scrawny, slender, often arching shrubs, 1–2.5 meters high . . . .**A. sanguinea** and **A. amabilis**
  2. Teeth of the leaves fine (5–12 per cm.); veins irregular, unequally distant, usually with frequent intermediate ones.
    4. Leaves rounded at apex; (shrubs in clumps or clusters).
      5. Leaves oval; stoloniferous shrubs, .5–1 meter high . . . . . .**A. stolonifera**
      5. Leaves oblong; shrubs forming clumps, about 2–8 meters high.
                                                              A. canadensis
    4. Leaves acute or short acuminate.
      6. Leaves acute; shrubs forming clumps . . . .**A. intermedia**
      6. Leaves short acuminate; trees or tall shrubs.
        7. Leaves pubescent, at least along their midribs or petioles.
                                                      A. arborea
        7. Leaves glabrous from the beginning . . . .**A. laevis**

Aralia—*Hercules Club and Sarsaparilla*

1. Stems spiny, forming tall shrubs or trees; leaves very large, often decompound . . . .**A. spinosa**
1. Stems bristly, somewhat woody, 4–9 dm. high; leaves twice-compound.
                                                      A. hispida

Aristolochia—*Dutchman's Pipe*

1. Leaves glabrate; winter twigs glabrous, stout, greenish; large vessels not clearly visible in cross-section of stem . . . .**A. durior**

1. Leaves tomentose; winter twigs finely pubescent, slender, glaucous, blue-green; large vessels clearly visible in cross-section of stem ......**A. tomentosa**

Ascyrum—*St. Peter's-wort*

1. Branchlets stout, erect; leaves thick, ovate to oblong, somewhat clasping at base ....**A. stans**
1. Branchlets slender; leaves thin, linear-oblong to linear-oblanceolate, contracted at base ....**A. hypericoides**

Berberis—*Barberries*

1. Leaves pinnately-compound, persistent ....**B. Aquifolium**
1. Leaves simple, deciduous.
    2. Margin of leaves entire; twigs reddish-brown to purple; spines simple or with two small lateral branches; compact low shrubs; fruits solitary.
    B. Thunbergii
    2. Margin of leaves serrate or dentate; twigs gray, orange-brown, or buff; spines branched, of three nearly equal parts; tall shrubs; fruits in drooping racemes ....**B. vulgaris**

Betula—*Birches*
Summer Key

1. Leaves obovate, orbicular or reniform, with rounded apex, margin crenate-dentate; shrubs.
    2. Twigs pubescent, not warty ....**B. pumila**
    2. Twigs glabrous or puberulent, glandular-warty ....**B. glandulosa**
1. Leaves ovate or at least with acute or tapering apex, margin usually doubly serrate; trees.
    3. Twigs glandular-warty; bark of trunk white; leaves mostly with less than eight pairs of veins.
        4. Apex of leaves long-tapering; petioles 2–3 cm. long; bark of trunk not peeling in layers ....**B. populifolia**
        4. Apex of leaves acuminate; petioles 1–3 cm. long; bark of trunk peeling in thin papery layers.
            5. Branchlets pendulous on older trees ....**B. pendula**
            5. Branchlets not pendulous ....**B. papyrifera**
    3. Twigs not glandular-warty; bark of trunk not white; leaves with seven or more pairs of veins.
        6. Lower surface of leaves, petioles, and twigs velvety-hairy; bark of twigs without wintergreen flavor ....**B. nigra**
        6. Lower surface of leaves not velvety-hairy; bark of twigs with wintergreen flavor.
            7. Leaves with lateral veins without prominent branches; bark of trunk peeling in thin layers ....**B. lutea**
            7. Leaves with lateral veins often with prominent branches; bark solid, not peeling ....**B. lenta**

Winter Key

1. Bark dark brown; buds 2–4 mm. long, obtuse, appressed, or ascending; shrubs.
     2. Twigs very rough glandular-warty ....**B. glandulosa**
     2. Twigs not glandular, usually pubescent ....**B. pumila**
1. Bark variously colored; buds 5–9 mm. long (or if smaller then acute); trees.
     3. Buds conspicuously flattened and appressed, quadrangular in cross-section; staminate catkins slender, clustered; bark of upper trunk reddish-brown or pink, exfoliating in thin papery layers; fruit on stout, erect, tomentose peduncles ....**B. nigra**
     3. Buds divergent or ascending, nearly terete.
         4. Buds conspicuously gummy within; outer scales often with resinous exudations; twigs without wintergreen flavor; bark white; pistillate catkins pendant or spreading, on slender stalks.
             5. Branchlets pendulous; bark separating into film-like layers. .**B. pendula**
             5. Branchlets not pendulous.
                 6. Twigs very rough glandular-warty; staminate catkins usually solitary; scales of pistillate catkins pubescent; bark dull chalky-white, not separating into film-like layers; stems usually in clumps; the lateral branches on each stem from near the ground, with black triangular spots below their insertion on the trunk ....**B. populifolia**
                 6. Twigs mostly pubescent but not rough glandular-warty; staminate catkins usually clustered; bark lustrous, separating into thin, film-like papery layers; stems usually solitary ....**B. papyrifera**
         4. Buds not conspicuously gummy within; young leaves in bud white-silky; twigs with wintergreen flavor; bark not white; pistillate catkins erect, oblong-ovoid, nearly sessile.
             7. Buds glabrous (lower scale occasionally ciliate), sharply divergent or recurved falcate; twigs glabrous, glossy reddish-brown; staminate catkins narrowly cylindrical, 3–3.5 mm. in diameter; pistillate catkins ovoid; scales glabrous; bark close, dark reddish-brown or black, broken into irregular plates on older trunks ....**B. lenta**
             7. Buds pubescent or at least with heavily ciliated scales, mostly ascending or slightly divergent; twigs somewhat pubescent, buff or yellowish-brown; staminate catkins rather broadly cylindrical, 4–5 mm. in diameter; pistillate catkins oblong, scales pubescent; bark buff or dirty yellow, separating into thin, film-like papery layers ....**B. lutea**

Calycanthus—*Carolina Allspice*

1. Lower surface of leaves very hairy; twigs with scattered hairs; leaf-scars somewhat sloping ....**C. floridus**
1. Lower surface of leaves glabrous or nearly so except along the veins; twigs minutely puberulent; leaf-scars shelflike ....**C. fertilis**

Carya—*Hickories*

Summer Key

1. Leaves mostly with more than 9 (9–17) leaflets; husk of fruit thin; shell of nut thin . . . .**C. pecan**
1. Leaves mostly with fewer than 9 (5–9) leaflets.
   2. Leaflets mostly 5–7.
      3. Rhachis and lower surface of midrib covered with clusters of hairs and silvery scales; husk of fruit thin . . . .**C. pallida**
      3. Rhachis and midrib not as above; husk of fruit thick.
         4. Terminal leaflet much larger than the upper pair of lateral leaflets; shell of nut thin . . . .**C. ovata**
         4. Terminal leaflet about the same size as the upper pair of lateral leaflets; shell of nut thick . . . .**C. glabra**
   2. Leaflets mostly 7–9.
      5. Buds yellow; husk of fruit thin; shell of nut thin . . . .**C. cordiformis**
      5. Buds not yellow; shell of nut thick.
         6. Leaves stellate-pubescent on the lower surface; husk of fruit thick.
             C. tomentosa
         6. Leaves not stellate-pubescent on the lower surface.
            7. Mature leaves pubescent; husk of fruit thick . . . .**C. laciniosa**
            7. Mature leaves glabrous or nearly so; husk of fruit thin . . . . .**C. ovalis**

Winter Key

1. Bud-scales 4–6 in pairs, valvate; bark of trunk close, not separating in strips
   2. Bud-scales yellow, glandular . . . .**C. cordiformis**
   2. Bud-scales with clusters of bright yellow hairs . . . .**C. pecan**
1. Bud-scales numerous, imbricated.
   3. Terminal bud 1–2.5 cm. long; twigs stout.
      4. Outer bud-scales early deciduous; terminal bud broadly ovate; bark of trunk rough and close, not separating in long strips or plates **C. tomentosa**
      4. Outer bud-scales persistent; terminal bud elongate-ovate; bark of trunk separating in long strips or plates.
         5. Twigs gray, olive, or red-brown . . . .**C. ovata**
         5. Twigs buff or orange . . . .**C. laciniosa**
   3. Terminal bud small, usually less than 1.5 cm. long; twigs slender.
      6. Buds puberulous; bud-scales silvery; bark of trunk rough-furrowed.
          C. pallida
      6. Buds glabrous or puberulent; bud-scales brown, red-brown, or greenish.
         7. Bark of trunk close furrowed; bud-scales green, sometimes puberulent.
             C. glabra
         7. Bark of trunk ridged, separating into plate-like scales . . . .**C. ovalis**

Castanea—*Chestnut*

1. Mature leaves white downy on lower surface; buds downy; shrubs or small trees ....**C. pumila**
1. Mature leaves glabrous and green on lower surface; buds glabrous; tall trees.
C. dentata

Catalpa—*Catalpa*

1. Bark of trunk thin, scaly; leaves usually abruptly acuminate; trees with low spreading crown; capsule less than 1 cm. thick ....**C. bignonioides**
1. Bark of trunk thick, ridged; leaves long-acuminate; trees with tall slender crown; capsule more than 1 cm. thick ....**C. speciosa**

Ceanothus—*New Jersey Tea*

1. Apex of leaf acute or acuminate; leaves usually ovate; twigs covered with orange, glandular excretions ....**C. americanus**
1. Apex of leaf obtuse or rounded; leaves usually elliptic-lanceolate; twigs nearly terete, warty ....**C. ovatus**

Celtis—*Hackberry, Sugarberry*

1. Leaf margin sharply serrate, at least above the middle; base obliquely rounded; bud-scales pubescent ....**C. occidentalis**
1. Leaf margin entire or nearly so; base obliquely crenate; bud-scales puberulent.
C. laevigata

Chimaphila—*Prince's Pine*

1. Leaf-base obtuse; upper surface of leaf marked with white veins or spots.
C. maculata
1. Leaf-base acute; upper surface of leaf without white veins or spots.
C. umbellata

Clematis—*Clematis, Virgin's Bower*

1. Flowers or clusters of achenes solitary on naked peduncles; leaves sometimes whorled ....**C. verticillaris**
1. Flowers or clusters of achenes in cymose clusters on branched leafy stalks; leaves opposite ....**C. virginiana**

Clethra—*Sweet Pepperbush*

1. Leaf-blades 3–10 cm. long, widest above the middle, glaucous or nearly so; racemes of capsules usually in erect panicles; bark of older stems gray or blackish-brown, often flaking; pubescence of twigs appressed .....**C. alnifolia**
1. Leaf-blades 7–15 cm. long, not widened above the middle; racemes of capsules usually solitary, flexuous, drooping; bark of older stems reddish-brown, exfoliating in thin strips; pubescence of twigs loose ....**C. acuminata**

Cornus—*Dogwoods*

By W. E. Manning

Summer Key

1. Leaves alternate, crowded near the ends of twigs; arborescent; fruit blue.
   C. alternifolia
1. Leaves opposite.
    2. Pubescence on twigs, petioles, or lower surface of leaves partly spreading, often woolly.
        3. Leaves very broadly ovate, with 6–8 pairs of lateral veins; very densely woolly pubescent below; twigs streaked with dark purple; fruit in cymes, bluish ....**C. rugosa**
        3. Leaves lanceolate to broadly ovate, with 3–5 (rarely 6) pairs of veins; twigs not streaked.
            4. Leaves broadly ovate, with 5–6 pairs of lateral veins; twigs appressed pubescent, usually glaucous; lateral branches longer than main axis; trees; fruit in dense heads, red ....**C. florida**
            4. Leaves ovate, with 3–4 pairs of veins; twigs usually spreading pubescent in part, not glaucous; lateral branches shorter than the main axis; shrubs; fruit in loose cymes.
                5. Leaves scabrous above, (woolly below); branchlets and branches grayish or light brown; pith variable, white or brown; fruit white.
                   C. asperifolia
                5. Leaves smooth or nearly so above; branchlets and branches purple (often becoming olive or gray later); pith in branchlets and branches uniform.
                    6. Pith white; pubescence between veins on lower surface of leaves woolly; fruit white ....**C. stolonifera ***
                    6. Pith brown; pubescence on veins on lower surface of leaves spreading, but between veins mostly appressed; fruit bluish.
                       C. Amomum
    2. Pubescence appressed or lacking, not woolly.
        7. Branches and branchlets reddish-purple (rarely olive); pith white; leaves glaucous below; fruit in cymes, white ....**C. stolonifera**
        7. Branches, and usually also branchlets, gray; pith white or brown; leaves pale or green below, not glaucous.
            8. Leaves broadly ovate; lateral buds divaricate; lateral branchlets often short (2-leaved), nearly at right angles to the branch; fruit solitary or in umbels, red ....**C. mas**
            8. Leaves elliptical to ovate lanceolate (3–4 pairs of veins); lateral buds appressed; lateral branchlets elongated, at acute angle; fruit in cymes or panicles, white, on red pedicels ....**C. racemosa**

Winter Key

1. Leaf-scars alternate, mostly crowded near the ends of twigs.
                                                    C. alternifolia
1. Leaf-scars opposite.
    2. Twigs and branchlets green or reddish-brown, streaked or speckled with dark purple ....**C. rugosa**
    2. Twigs and branchlets uniform in color, not streaked with purple.
        3. Lateral buds hidden behind the raised leaf-scars; enlarged depressed-globose flower buds often present, about 5–8 mm. in diameter; twigs usually glaucous, terete, or flattened ....**C. florida**
        3. Lateral buds distinctly visible.
            4. Lateral buds divergent; enlarged globose flower buds often present; twigs usually green ....**C. mas**
            4. Lateral buds appressed; flower buds not prominently enlarged.
                5. Twigs and branchlets bright reddish purple; lenticels few (8–20 per internode), separate and conspicuous on twigs, branchlets and branches; pith pure white; (stems stoloniferous) .... **C. stolonifera** *
                5. Twigs and branchlets dull purple, brown, or gray; lenticels often apparently absent, (when conspicuous on twigs, numerous and minute, often confluent on branchlets).
                    6. Lenticels prominent but minute on twigs and branchlets; twigs light brown; branchlets gray; pith white or pale brown; (pubescence appressed) ....**C. racemosa**
                    6. Lenticels apparently absent on most twigs, becoming abundant on branchlets; pubescence spreading.
                        7. Twigs and branchlets purple; 3–4 year branchlets often streaked by confluent lenticels; pith brown ....**C. Amomum**
                        7. Twigs reddish-brown; branchlets and branches light brown or gray, rarely streaked; pith white or brown ......**C. asperifolia**
C. alba has blunter leaves and more erect non-stoloniferous stems.

Corylus—*Hazelnuts*

1. Bud-scales imbricated, several scales shorter than the bud; staminate catkins usually evidently stalked; twigs often coarsely glandular-pubescent; husk of fruit not elongated ....**C. americana**
1. Bud-scales, except the two lower ones, as long as the bud; staminate catkins sessile or nearly so; twigs mostly glabrous; husk of fruit elongated into a tube.
                                                    C. cornuta

Cupressaceae—*Cedars, Arbor-Vitae, Junipers, etc.*

1. Branchlets and small branches in two ranks, forming a flattened spray.
    2. Leaves in whorls of four (with long internodes; cones elongated, with thin scales) ....**Libocedrus decurrens**
    2. Leaves opposite or in whorls of three.
        3. Leaves on the lower side of branchlets with broad stomate-bearing areas, one on the center of each lateral leaf and two on the median leaf; margins of each pair of opposite leaves forming a V-shaped line.
            4. Leaves thin, very acute, appressed or spreading, glandular on back; spray mostly very glaucous beneath; cones nearly globose, with radiating peltate scales ....**Chamaecyparis pisifera**
            4. Leaves thick, mostly obtuse, appressed; spray not or but slightly glaucous beneath; cones oblong with ascending non-peltate scales.
                5. Leaves strongly glandular with raised oval glands; stomate-bearing areas distinct ....**Thuja occidentalis**
                5. Leaves indistinctly or not at all glandular.
                    6. Spray regularly pinnately-branched; stomate-bearing areas distinct; glands scarcely visible ....**Thuja plicata**
                    6. Spray irregularly branched.
                        7. Branchlets 2.5–4 mm. broad; stomate-bearing areas distinct; glands usually invisible; cone-scales thin ......**Thuja Standishii**
                        7. Branchlets 1–2 mm. broad, arranged in vertical planes; stomate-bearing areas of scattered white stomates; glands usually visible; cone-scales thick ....**Thuja orientalis**
        3. Leaves without broad stomate-bearing areas; stomates indistinct; leaves green, glaucous or with glaucous margin; the glands obscure; cones subglobose, with peltate scales.
            8. Branchlets weakly carinate above and below; leaves closely appressed, the margins of opposite pairs forming a V-shaped line, or with acute spreading tips. ....**Chamaecyparis nootkatensis**
            8. Branchlets not carinate; leaves obtuse, closely appressed, margins of leaves forming white Y-shaped lines on lower side of branchlets.
                Chamaecyparis obtusa
1. Branchlets and small branches not in two ranks, extending more or less in all directions, spray not flattened.
    9. Leaves all scale-like.
        10. Trees; leaves with a prominent raised gland on the back, mostly appressed; spray consisting of small fascicled, irregularly fan-shaped portions; fruit a cone with peltate scales ......**Chamaecyparis thyoides**
        10. Plants decumbent, often creeping; leaves acutely cuspidate, with a gland on the back; fruit a "berry" ....**Juniperus horizontalis**

9. Leaves, at least some of them, strongly subulate, the others scale-like; shrubs or trees.
  11. Leaves in whorls of three, jointed at base, not decurrent, spreading, prickly pointed, channeled and glaucous above; with winter buds; fruit a "berry."
    12. Trees about 2–4 meters high ....Juniperus communis
    12. Plants decumbent, forming mats 3–10 dm. high.
                            Juniperus communis var. depressa
  11. Leaves opposite or rarely whorled, scale-like and imbricated or subulate, loose and prickly pointed on young shoots, decurrent but not jointed; without winter buds.
    13. Leaves mostly scale-like and imbricated; fruit a berry.
      14. Erect trees or shrubs ....Juniperus virginiana
      14. Prostrate or creeping ....Juniperus horizontalis
    13. Leaves subulate, often remote and spreading. Juvenile forms of various genera known as *Retinospora* may key out to here.

Elaeagnus—*Oleaster*

1. Leaves, twigs, and buds covered with silvery scales ....E. angustifolia
1. Leaves, twigs, and buds covered with brown scales and silvery scales.
                            E. argentea

Evonymus—*Burning Bush*

1. Stems climbing by means of roots ....E. fortunei
1. Stems not climbing.
  2. Twigs with corky wings ....E. alata
  2. Twigs without corky wings.
    3. Petioles 1–5 mm. long; twigs square in cross-section; stems trailing, rooting at the nodes, or low bushes; fruit red, warty.
      4. Leaves obovate, thick, dull green, apex often obtuse; trailing shrubs.
                            E. obovata
      4. Leaves ovate to lanceolate, thin, bright green, apex acute; erect or stoloniferous shrubs ... . E. americana
    3. Petioles 1–3 cm. long; twigs terete; stems erect, tall shrubs or small trees; fruit smooth.
      5. Lower leaf-surface usually puberulent; fruit purple ....E. atropurpurea
      5. Lower leaf-surface glabrous; fruit pink ....E. europaea

Forsythia—*Golden Bells*

1. Pith hollow or chambered throughout ....**F. viridissima**
1. Pith solid at the nodes.
    2. Pith more or less chambered in the internodes ....**F. intermedia**
    2. Pith hollow in the internodes ....**F. suspensa**

Fraxinus—*Ashes*

Summer Key

1. Twigs acutely four-angled at internodes ....**F. quadrangulata**
1. Twigs terete or obtusely angled.
    2. Twigs and petioles pubescent or tomentose.
        3. Twigs and petioles pubescent ....**F. pennsylvanica**
        3. Twigs and petioles tomentose ....**F. tomentosa**
    2. Twigs and petioles glabrous or nearly so.
        4. Lateral leaflets sessile, commonly ten.
            5. Leaf rhachis tomentose at base of leaflets ....**F. nigra**
            5. Leaf rhachis glabrous ....**F. excelsior**
        4. Lateral leaflets stalked, commonly six.
            6. Leaflets elliptic-oval ....**F. americana**
            6. Leaflets elliptic-lanceolate ....**F. pennsylvanica** var. **lanceolata**

Winter Key

1. Twigs acutely four-angled; buds gray, woolly ....**F. quadrangulata**
1. Twigs terete or obtusely angled; buds brown to black.
    2. Upper margin of leaf-scars deeply concave, or with a sharply V-shaped notch; twigs smooth and mostly glossy; terminal bud usually rounded, dome-shaped.
        3. Twigs tomentose; fruit with wing decurrent to middle or more
                                          F. tomentosa
        3. Twigs glabrous; fruit with apical wing ....**F. americana**
    2. Upper margin of leaf-scars convex, straight, or seldom very slightly concave.
        4. Lateral buds nearly globose.
            5. Buds blue-black; terminal bud mostly obtuse or rounded at apex, dome-shaped; twigs somewhat glossy, mostly green ....**F. excelsior**
            5. Buds black or sometimes brown; terminal bud acute at apex; twigs dull, grayish, with conspicuous lenticels; (bark on older branches corky) ....**F. nigra**
        4. Lateral buds reniform in anterior view and also compressed parallel to the surface of the twig, appressed, brown; twigs glossy or velvety; (lenticels often raised and conspicuous).
            6. Twigs velvety ....**F. pennsylvanica**
            6. Twigs glabrous or glabrate ....**F. pennsylvanica** var. **lanceolata**

Gaylussacia—*Huckleberries*
Summer Key

1. Leaves coriaceous, persistent, serrate, without resinous dots ....**G. brachycera**
1. Leaves not coriaceous, deciduous, usually entire and with resinous dots.
  2. Leaves green on both surfaces; apex mucronate ....**G. dumosa**
  2. Leaves glaucous or yellowish on the lower surface; apex not mucronate.
    3. Leaves finely pubescent and glaucous on lower surface; fruit glaucous.
      G. frondosa
    3. Leaves yellowish with resinous dots on lower surface; fruit not glaucous.
      G. baccata

Winter Key

1. Leaves persistent ....**G. brachycera**
1. Leaves deciduous.
  2. Twigs glaucous ....**G. frondosa**
  2. Twigs not glaucous, usually pubescent.
    3. Exposed bud-scales 2–3 ....**G. baccata**
    3. Exposed bud-scales 4–5 ....**G. dumosa**

Gleditsia—*Honey Locust*

1. Thorns branched; legume linear, 10 cm. long or more, pulpy, more than 3-seeded ....**G. triacanthos**
1. Thorns mostly simple; legume oval, about 3–4 cm. long, not pulpy, 1–3-seeded ....**G. aquatica**

Hudsonia—*Hudsonia*

1. Plant hoary with down; leaves appressed, oval or oblong, 2 mm. long.
    H. tomentosa
1. Plant downy but green; leaves divaricate, subulate, 3–6 mm. long.
    H. ericoides

Hydrangea—*Hydrangea*

1. Leaves densely tomentose on lower surface; leaf-scars with 5–7 bundle-scars.
    H. cinerea
1. Leaves glabrous on lower surface or pubescent along veins; leaf-scars with three bundle-scars.
  2. Leaves opposite; buds conical, at right angles to the twigs; fruits in flat-topped clusters ....**H. arborescens**
  2. Leaves often whorled; buds elongated, appressed or pointing forward on twigs; fruits in conical clusters ....**H. paniculata** var. **grandiflora**

Hypericum—*St. John's-wort*

1. Branchlets four-angled; capsule five-celled ....**H. Kalmianum**
1. Branchlets two-angled; capsule three-celled.
  2. Leaves oblong to oblanceolate; capsule 1–1.5 cm. long ......**H. prolificum**
  2. Leaves linear-oblong to linear, revolute; capsule 5–8 mm. long.
    H. densiflorum

Ilex—*Holly*

1. Leaves coriaceous, persistent.
    2. Leaves with coarse spiny teeth; fruit red ....I. opaca
    2. Leaves serrate toward the apex; fruit black ....I. glabra
1. Leaves not coriaceous, deciduous.
    3. Nutlets ribbed on the back; leaves and fruits often on spurs.
        4. Margin of leaves crenate or bluntly serrate ....I. decidua
        4. Margin of leaves sharply and finely serrate ....I. montana
    3. Nutlets smooth and even on the back; leaves and fruits not on spurs.
        5. Leaves mostly ovate or obovate, margin serrate, downy on the lower surface, or with few hairs, chiefly along the veins ....I. verticillata
        5. Leaves mostly lanceolate or oblong-lanceolate, margin serrulate, mostly glabrous on the lower surface ....I. laevigata

Juglans—*Walnuts and Butternuts*

Summer Key

1. Margin of leaflets entire or remotely denticulate; leaves and twigs glabrous; pith light brown; bark smooth and gray ....J. regia
1. Margin of leaflets serrate; leaves and usually the twigs pubescent.
    2. Leaves smooth and glossy above; leaf-scars without a hairy fringe along the upper margin; pith light brown; bark light brown and rough .....J. nigra
    2. Leaves somewhat pubescent above; leaf-scar with a hairy fringe along the upper margin; bark of trunk gray, with broad ridges.
        3. Leaflets 1–1.5 dm. long; pith violet-brown; fruits in long racemes.
                                                                    J. Sieboldiana
        3. Leaflets usually less than 1 dm. long; pith dark brown; fruits in clusters of 3–5 ....J. cinerea

Winter Key

1. Leaf-scar with a hairy fringe along the upper margin; bark of trunk gray, with broad ridges.
    2. Pith dark brown, diaphragms thick, nearly as wide as the intervening chambers; upper margin of leaf-scar not conspicuously notched ....J. cinerea
    2. Pith light brown, diaphragms thin, much narrower than the intervening chambers; upper margin of leaf-scar conspicuously notched.
                                                                    J. Sieboldiana
1. Leaf-scar without a hairy fringe along the upper margin; pith light brown.
    3. Twigs glabrous and not sticky; buds glabrate; bark of trunk light gray, remaining smooth for a long time ....J. regia
    3. Twigs densely gray-downy and somewhat sticky at first; buds pubescent; bark of trunk dark brown, ridges narrow and broken cross-wise ...J. nigra

Kalmia—*Mountain Laurel*

1. Twigs two-edged; leaves opposite or in whorls of three, nearly sessile, white beneath ....**K. polifolia**
1. Twigs terete; leaves distinctly petioled; green on both sides.
   2. Leaves narrowly oblong, mostly obtuse, usually in whorls of three or opposite; fruits in lateral corymbs ....**K. angustifolia**
   2. Leaves elliptical or oval, acute at each end, alternate or some of them opposite or rarely whorled; fruits in terminal corymbs ....**K. latifolia**

Larix—*Larches or Tamaracks*

1. Cones less than 2 cm. long, with few scales; branchlets stiff, not drooping; twigs slender, light to yellowish-brown; bark of trunk shedding as small irregular scales ....**L. laricina**
1. Cones more than 2 cm. long, with many scales; branchlets pendulous from the lateral branches; twigs stouter, yellowish; bark of trunk shedding as large plate-like scales ....**L. decidua**

Leucothoë—*Fetter Bush*

1. Leaves taper-pointed; branches and racemes recurved-spreading....**L. recurva**
1. Leaves acute-pointed; branches and racemes mostly erect ....**L. racemosa**

Ligustrum—*Privet*

1. Twigs, buds and leaves glabrous; lateral buds with acuminate scales; leaves sometimes persistent ....**L. ovalifolium**
1. Twigs and buds pubescent or puberulous; lateral buds with blunt scales; leaves deciduous.
   2. Leaves, at least along the midrib, pubescent; twigs pubescent.
   L. obtusifolium
   2. Leaves glabrous; twigs puberulous ....**L. vulgare**

Lindera (*Benzoin*) *Spice Bush*

1. Leaves, twigs and buds glabrous or glabrate ....**L. Benzoin**
1. Leaves, twigs and buds pubescent ....**L. melissaefolium**

Lonicera—*Honeysuckles*

1. Twining or trailing vines.
   2. Leaves green on both surfaces, ciliate; twigs hairy.
      3. Leaves persistent, not connate; berry black ....**L. japonica**
      3. Leaves deciduous, the upper connate; berry red ....**L. hirsuta**
   2. Leaves glaucous, at least on the lower surface; the upper leaves of flower shoots connate; twigs glabrous or nearly so; berry red or orange.
      4. Leaves glaucous on both upper and lower surface ....**L. prolifera**
      4. Leaves green on the upper surface.
         5. Twigs glaucous ....**L. dioica**
         5. Twigs not glaucous ....**L. sempervirens**

1. Erect shrubs; upper leaves not connate; fruit in pairs on axillary peduncles.
  6. Pith of branchlets white, solid between the nodes.
    7. Leaves thin, ovate-oblong, ciliate; buds conical; bud-scales not long-acuminate; twigs flexuous and spreading ....**L. canadensis**
    7. Leaves thick, oblong to elliptical; buds four-sided; bud-scales long-acuminate; twigs stiff, ascending.
      8. Leaves tapering at base, glabrous or nearly so; bark grayish; berry red or purple; slender, erect shrubs ....**L. oblongifolia**
      8. Leaves rounded at base, hairy on both surfaces, ciliate; bark of branchlets brown, much shredding; berry bluish-black; low shrubs or mats.
                                       L. caerulea
  6. Pith of branchlets dark, hollow between the nodes.
    9. Leaves, buds and twigs glabrous or nearly so; buds ovoid; winter twigs gray or yellow-brown ....**L. tatarica**
    9. Leaves and buds hairy.
      10. Buds fusiform, with ciliate pubescent scales; twigs puberulent, dirty-gray ....**L. Xylosteum**
      10. Buds short-conical, obtuse, glabrescent; twigs soft-pubescent, spreading ....**L. Morrowi**

Lyonia—*Staggerbush*

1. Leaves serrate; visible bud-scales two, the inner white-silky; buds oblong-acute, closely appressed; winter twigs greenish-yellow, pubescent, at least near tip; capsule globose ....**L. ligustrina**
1. Leaves entire; visible bud-scales 4–5, the inner glabrous; buds conical, divergent; winter twigs brown, glabrous; capsules urn-shaped ......**L. mariana**

Magnolia—*Magnolias*

Summer Key

1. Lower surface of leaves and twigs rusty-tomentose; leaves glossy on upper surface, coriaceous, and persistent ....**M. grandiflora**
1. Lower surface of leaves not rusty-tomentose.
  2. Leaves scattered along the twigs; leaf buds hairy; terminal bud hairy or silky white.
    3. Lower surface of leaves glaucous; leaves 7–16 cm. long, often persistent.
                                      M. virginiana
    3. Lower surface of leaves not glaucous.
      4. Lower surface of leaves white, strongly pubescent; leaves 3–9 dm. long.
                                   M. macrophylla
      4. Lower surface of leaves green, slightly pubescent; leaves 1–2.5 dm. long ....**M. acuminata**
  2. Leaves 1 to 6 dm. long, crowded near the end of the twigs; leaf buds glabrous; terminal bud glaucous purple.
    5. Leaf-base tapering ....**M. tripetala**
    5. Leaf-base auriculate ....**M. Fraseri**

Winter Key

1. Leaves persistent.
    2. Lower surface of leaves and twigs rusty-tomentose ....**M. grandiflora**
    2. Lower surface of leaves glaucous; twigs glabrous, green .....**M. virginiana**
1. Leaves deciduous.
    3. Leaf buds hairy; terminal bud hairy or silky, white; leaf-scars scattered along the twigs.
        4. Terminal bud 3–5 cm. long; twigs brown, very stout ....**M. macrophylla**
        4. Terminal bud 1–2 cm. long.
            5. Terminal bud covered with fine silky hairs or glabrous; twigs green.
            M. virginiana
            5. Terminal bud covered with long white hairs; twigs brown.
            M. acuminata
    3. Leaf buds glabrous; terminal bud glaucous, purple; leaf-scars crowded near end of annual growth.
        6. Terminal bud 2–3 cm. long; leaf-scars with minute resin glands on surface; two-year old branchlets brown, very stout; bark light gray.
        M. tripetala
        6. Terminal bud 3–5 cm. long; leaf-scars without resin glands; two-year old branchlets gray, slender; bark brown ....**M. Fraseri**

Morus—*Mulberries*

1. Leaves glabrous and glossy above; lobes, if present, rounded; buds appressed, more or less flattened, mostly less than 4 mm. long; bud-scales reddish-brown, without darker margins; bark yellowish-brown ....**M. alba**
1. Leaves rough on upper surface and downy on lower surface; lobes, if present, pointed; buds divergent, not at all or but slightly flattened, mostly more than 5 mm. long; bud-scales greenish-brown, with darker margins; bark dark brown ....**M. rubra**

Myrica—*Bayberries and Sweet Fern*

Summer Key

1. Leaves pinnately lobed; nuts in bur-like catkins ....**M. peregrina**
1. Leaves entire or serrate.
    2. Leaves pale green and with small resinous dots at least on the lower surface; nuts two-winged, in cone-like catkins ....**M. Gale**

2. Leaves bright green and with prominent resinous dots; nuts scattered, encrusted with white wax.
   3. Leaves mostly .8–1.5 cm. broad and with acute apex; resinous dots common on both surfaces; nuts 2.5–3 mm. in diameter . . . . **M. cerifera**
   3. Leaves mostly 1.5–4 cm. broad and with obtuse apex; resinous dots often scarce or absent on the upper surface; nuts 3.5–4 mm. in diameter.
M. pennsylvanica

Winter Key

1. Stipule-scars present . . . .**M. peregrina**
1. Stipule-scars absent; (large catkin-like flower buds often present).
  2. Terminal bud absent; lateral buds conical-ovoid or oblong; nut two-winged, not waxy . . . . **M. Gale**
  2. Terminal bud present; lateral buds subglobose, obtuse; nut encrusted with wax.
   3. Buds yellow-glandular, 1 mm. long . . . .**M. cerifera**
   3. Buds not yellow-glandular, 1.5 mm. long; with catkin-like flower-buds.
M. pennsylvanica

Parthenocissus—Virginia Creeper

1. Leaves simple or trifoliate . . . .**P. tricuspidata**
1. Leaves palmately five-foliate.
  2. Tendrils tipped with expanded discs . . . .**P. quinquefolia**
  2. Tendrils mostly without expanded discs . . . . **P. vitacea**

Philadelphus—Syringa

1. Bark of branchlets gray, not exfoliating . . . .**P. pubescens**
1. Bark of branchlets light brown, exfoliating in thin flakes . . . . . .**P. grandiflorus**
(Most of the cultivated Syringas are hybrids.)

Picea—Spruces

1. Twigs pubescent; cone-scales stiff.
  2. Lateral branchlets long and pendulous; leaves dark green, sharp-pointed; cones cylindrical, 10–18 cm. long . . . .**P. Abies**
  2. Lateral branchlets not or slightly pendulous; leaves blunt; cones subglobose, 2–5 cm. long.
   3. Leaves bluish-green, dull; hairs on twigs tipped with glands; cones persisting many years; cone-scales denticulate . . . .**P. mariana**
   3. Leaves dark yellowish-green, lustrous; hairs on twigs without glands; cones usually persisting only one year; cone-scales entire or nearly so.
P. rubens
1. Twigs glabrous or nearly so; cone-scales stiff or flexible; cones cylindrical.
  4. Leaves dark green.

5. Twigs reddish-brown; lateral branchlets long and pendulous; cones 10–18 cm. long, their scales stiff ....**P. Abies**

5. Twigs mostly yellow-brown or gray; lateral branchlets stiff; cones 3–5 cm. long, their scales thin and flexible ....**P. glauca**

4. Leaves blue-green or silvery-white; cone-scales thin and flexible.

   6. Leaves very sharp-pointed; cones 3–8 cm. long ....**P. pungens**

   6. Leaves blunt or sharp-pointed; cones 3–5 cm. long ....**P. glauca**

Pinus—*Pines*

1. Leaves five (rarely more) in a cluster; sheaths of leaf clusters deciduous; cones cylindrical, their scales thin. (Soft pines.)

  2. Branchlets densely brownish tomentose; cones 6–9 cm. long ......**P. cembra**

  2. Branchlets not as above, glabrous or hairy.

    3. Leaves 1.5–2 dm. long, flaccid and drooping; branchlets glaucous; cones 1.5–2.5 dm. long ....**P. Griffithsii**

    3. Leaves .7–1.3 dm. long; branchlets not glaucous.

      4. Branchlets glabrous or pubescent, greenish or light greenish-brown; leaves flexible; cones 1–2 dm. long ....**P. strobus**

      4. Branchlets puberulent, yellowish or reddish-brown; leaves stiff; cones 1.3–3 dm. long ....**P. monticola**

1. Leaves two or three in a cluster; sheaths of leaf clusters persistent; cone-scales thick, mostly armed with spines. (Pitch pines.)

  5. Leaves mostly three in a cluster, cone-scales armed with spines.

    6. Young cones lateral.

      7. Leaves .7–1.2 dm. long, yellow-green, stout; cones 3–10 cm. long, persistent for many years ....**P. rigida**

      7. Leaves 1.5–3 dm. long, pale green or glaucous, slender; cones 5–15 cm. long, not long persistent ....**P. taeda**

    6. Young cones subterminal.

      8. Leaves stout, stiff, 1–3 dm. long; buds red; cones .7–1.5 dm. long.
                             P. ponderosa

      8. Leaves slender, pendulous, 2–4.5 dm. long; buds white; cones 1.5–2.5 dm. long ....**P. palustris**

  5. Leaves mostly two in a cluster.

    9. Branchlets glaucous; cones lateral; cone-scales with or without spines.

      10. Leaves stout, gray-green, 4–8 cm. long; buds very resinous; cones about 8 cm. long ....**P. virginiana**

      10. Leaves slender, dark blue-green, 8–13 cm. long; buds slightly or not at all resinous; cones about 5 cm. long ....**P. echinata**

    9. Branchlets not glaucous.

      11. Leaves 8–24 cm. long; cones subterminal, at right angles to the branch, symmetrical, the scales without spines.

12. Leaves lustrous, slender, soft and flexible; bark of trunk reddish; cones 4–6 cm. long ....**P. resinosa**

12. Leaves dull, stout, stiff, and sharp-pointed; bark of trunk gray; cones 5–9 cm. long ....**P. nigra** var. **austriaca**

11. Leaves 2–9 cm. long, stout.

13. Branchlets dull greenish-yellow or yellow-brown; resin ducts in leaves near the surface; cones unsymmetrical, recurved.

14. Branchlets dull greenish-yellow; leaves bluish-green, twisted; trees; bark on upper trunk reddish; cones 3–5 cm. long ....**P. sylvestris**

14. Branchlets usually yellow-brown; leaves dark or yellow-green, slightly or not at all twisted; shrubs; bark on upper trunk dark gray; cones 2–5 cm. long ....**P. Mugo**

13. Branchlets orange or orange-brown; resin ducts medial; leaves mostly stiff and twisted; cones symmetrical or unsymmetrical.

15. Leaves 2–4 cm. long; cones lateral, 3–5 cm. long, incurved, pointing forward; cone-scales mostly without spines ....**P. Banksiana**

15. Leaves 3–9 cm. long; cones not pointing forward; cone-scales armed with spines.

16. Leaves yellow-green, containing one or two resin ducts; cones subterminal, 3–5 cm. long, each scale with a slender spine ..**P. contorta**

16. Leaves dark blue-green, containing 2–5 resin ducts; cones lateral, 6–9 cm. long, each scale with a stout hooked spine ....**P. pungens**

Platanus—*Sycamore*

1. Lobes of leaves longer than broad; flower heads in racemes of three or more.
   P. orientalis

1. Lobes of leaves not longer than broad; flower heads one or two, rarely three, on a pendulous stalk.

2. Flower heads mostly solitary; lobes of leaves broader than long.
   P. occidentalis

2. Flower heads mostly two; middle lobe of leaf about as long as wide.
   P. acerifolia

Populus—*Poplars and Aspens*

Summer Key

1. Leaves white-tomentose on the lower surface, often lobed ....**P. alba**

1. Leaves not white-tomentose (when mature), not lobed.

2. Petioles round or grooved.

3. Leaves becoming rusty along the lower surface of veins; buds very resinous and scented.

4. Petioles and twigs pubescent; leaves mostly cordate ....**P. candicans**

4. Petioles and twigs glabrous or puberulous; leaves mostly ovate.
   P. tacamahaca

3. Leaves not becoming rusty along the lower surface of veins, broadly ovate with incurved glandular teeth; buds slightly resinous and scented.

P. heterophylla

2. Petioles flattened.
    5. Leaves dull or gray-green.
        6. Leaf margin finely dentate; buds glossy brown ....P. tremuloides
        6. Leaf margin coarsely dentate; buds gray pubescent ....P. grandidentata
    5. Leaves bright or yellow-green; buds not pubescent.
        7. Leaves with small teeth, slightly or not at all incurved, without glands; lateral buds appressed; branches strongly fastigiate.

P. nigra var. italica

        7. Leaves with strongly incurved callus teeth and two glands near top of petiole; lateral buds divergent ....P. deltoides

Winter Key

1. Buds downy or silky.
    2. Buds and younger twigs both white-downy ....P. alba
    2. Buds pale-downy; twigs glabrous or slightly downy ....P. grandidentata
1. Buds glabrous or resinous.
    3. Twigs yellow, yellowish-brown or olive-brown; buds not fragrant.
        4. Lateral buds appressed, mostly under 8 mm. long; tree fastigiate.

P. nigra var. italica

        4. Lateral buds divergent, usually 10 mm. or more long ....P. deltoides
    3. Twigs dark brown or reddish-brown.
        5. Buds small, less than 10 mm. long, glossy, slightly resinous but not fragrant.
            6. Margin of bud-scales scarious ....P. tremuloides
            6. Margin of bud-scales not scarious ....P. heterophylla
        5. Buds large, more than 15 mm. long, resinous, fragrant.
            7. Lateral buds with three visible scales; twigs hairy, at least at base.

P. candicans

            7. Lateral buds with two visible scales; twigs glabrous. .....P. tacamahaca

Prunus—*Plums and Cherries*
Summer Key

1. Plants dwarf shrubs, usually less than 1 meter high; (leaves spatulate-oblong, pale on the lower surface, distantly serrate) ....P. pumila
1. Plants trees or tall shrubs.
    2. Leaves downy on the lower surface; fruits solitary or a few in an umbel.
        3. Margin of leaves finely and evenly serrate ....P. maritima
        3. Margin of leaves coarsely and unevenly serrate ....P. domestica
    2. Leaves not downy on the lower surface.

4. Leaves lanceolate, oblong-lanceolate or elliptical.
     5. Leaves smooth and waxy on the lower surface, usually with prominent pubescence on the lower surface along both sides of the midrib; fruits in racemes ....**P. serotina**
     5. Leaves wrinkled and veiny, pubescence not as above.
         6. Margin of leaves finely or doubly serrate; fruits glabrous, in corymbs.
                 P. pennsylvanica
         6. Margin of leaves coarsely serrate or crenate-serrate; fruits pubescent, usually solitary ....**P. persica**
4. Leaves ovate, obovate or oblong-ovate.
     7. Leaves sharply serrate.
         8. Apex acuminate; stem often thorny; terminal bud absent; fruits solitary or in umbels ....**P. americana**
         8. Apex obtuse or acute; stem thornless; terminal bud present; fruits in racemes ....**P. virginiana**
     7. Leaves crenate, crenate-serrate or doubly serrate; fruits solitary or in umbels.
         9. Apex acuminate; stem often thorny; terminal bud absent......**P. nigra**
         9. Apex not acuminate; stem thornless; spurs present; terminal bud present.
             10. Lateral veins 6–8 on each side of midrib; fruit spurs leafy.
                 P. Cerasus
             10. Lateral veins 10–14 on each side of midrib; fruit spurs leafless.
                 P. avium

Winter Key

1. Terminal bud present.
     2. Buds woolly pubescent; (collateral buds often present; twigs green or red; lenticels prominent) ....**P. persica**
     2. Buds not woolly.
         3. Plants dwarf shrubs, usually less than 1 meter high ....**P. pumila**
         3. Plants trees or tall shrubs.
             4. Buds clustered at the ends of slender red twigs and short spurs; twigs glossy ....**P. pennsylvanica**
             4. Buds not clustered at the ends of both twigs and spurs, (clusters of buds present only at the end of spurs in some species, or if several buds are found at the end of slender twigs then the spurs are absent).
                 5. Flower buds present on older growth, mostly clustered at the end of short spurs.
                     6. Twigs stout; buds chestnut-brown; tree tall with persistent central stem; bark smooth, often peeling in rolls ....**P. avium**
                     6. Twigs slender; buds brown; tree low-branching without persistent central stem; bark rough, with small scales ....**P. Cerasus**
                 5. Flower buds and spurs absent.

7. Buds about 6 mm. long; scales rounded at apex, their margins light gray, covered part brown; twigs stout, light brown, dull; tall shrubs or small trees; bark smooth ....**P. virginiana**

7. Buds about 4 mm. long; scales blunt or pointed at apex, exposed part nearly uniform reddish-brown in color, covered part green or reddish; twigs slender or medium stout, reddish-brown, glossy; trees; bark rough and scaly on old trunks ....**P. serotina**

1. Terminal bud absent.
8. Buds velvety or puberulent, broadly ovoid; thorns rarely present.
9. Twigs glabrous; buds puberulent ....**P. domestica**
9. Twigs and buds velvety ....**P. maritima**
8. Buds glabrous, ovoid-fusiform; thorns usually present.
10. Buds black or gray, generally over 4 mm. long ....**P. nigra**
10. Buds red-brown, generally under 4 mm. long ....**P. americana**

Pyrus—*Apples etc.* Key to species, see page 77.

Quercus—*Oaks*

Summer Key

1. Lobes or teeth of the leaves blunt, or sometimes acute, not bristle-tipped; fruit maturing the first season; shell of the acorn glabrous on the inner surface.
(*White Oaks*)

2. Leaves pinnately lobed.
3. Leaves rough and stellate-pubescent on the upper surface, pubescent on the lower surface; with 5–7 lobes, the upper usually truncate or emarginate; acorn sessile or short-stalked ....**Q. stellata**
3. Leaves smooth, not stellate-pubescent on the upper surface.
4. Leaves glabrous on the lower surface.
5. Leaves distinctly stalked, base acute .... Q. alba
5. Leaves sessile or nearly so, base auriculate .... Q. robur
4. Leaves pubescent or tomentose on the lower surface.
6. Upper scales of the acorn cup long-awned ....Q. macrocarpa
6. Upper scales of the acorn cup not awned ....Q. lyrata
2. Leaves coarsely and regularly sinuate-toothed.
7. Leaves with acutely pointed teeth.
8. Leaves with 3–7 teeth on each side ....Q. prinoides
8. Leaves with 8–13 teeth on each side.
9. Outline of blade lanceolate to oblong ....Q. Muhlenbergia
9. Outline of blade obovate to oval ....Q. Michauxii
7. Leaves with rounded or crenate teeth.
10. Fruit sessile or nearly so; scales of acorn cup not awned ......Q. Prinus
10. Fruit long-peduncled; upper scales of acorn cup more or less awned.
Q. bicolor

1. Leaves or their sharp lobes or teeth bristle-tipped; fruit maturing the second season; shell of the acorn tomentose on the inner surface ....(*Black Oaks*)
11. Leaves entire.
12. Leaves glabrous, linear-lanceolate to lanceolate ....Q. phellos

12. Leaves pubescent on the lower surface, oblong-lanceolate to oblong-obovate .... **Q. imbricaria**

11. Leaves not entire.

   13. Leaves broad-obovate, often dilated at the wide, obscurely lobed apex, lower surface light brown .... **Q. marilandica**

   13. Leaves pinnately lobed.

      14. Leaves whitish or grayish on the lower surface.

         15. Lobes of leaves broadly triangular .... **Q. ilicifolia**

         15. Lobes of leaves elongated, the upper falcate .... **Q. rubra**

      14. Leaves green on both surfaces.

         16. Leaves usually dull on the upper surface; lobes 4–6 on each side, broadest at base; length of largest lobes less than or equalling the width of blade between bases of lobes .... **Q. borealis***

         16. Leaves usually lustrous on the upper surface; lobes 2–5 on each side, length of largest lobes usually two to several times the width of blade between bases of lobes.

            17. Upper scales of the acorn cup pubescent, loosely imbricated; sinuses widest at the outside .... **Q. velutina**

            17. Upper scales of the acorn cup glabrous or nearly so, closely appressed; sinuses contracted at the outside or of same width throughout.

               18. Nut of acorn ellipsoidal, covered for one third its length by a cup with tapering base; leaves turning brown in autumn.

                                            Q. ellipsoidalis

               18. Nut of acorn globose or hemispherical; leaves turning scarlet in autumn.

                  19. Acorn cup saucer-shaped .... **Q. palustris**

                  19. Acorn cup hemispheric .... **Q. coccinea**

Winter Key

1. Fruit maturing the second season; shell of acorn mostly hairy on the inner surface; acorn cups sessile or short-stalked .... (*Black Oaks*)

  2. Buds large; terminal ones usually over 4.5 mm. long.

     3. Buds covered with dense wool, prominently angled; bark of trunk black, rough, with deep fissures and irregular ridges which are broken crosswise; acorn cups top-shaped to hemispheric.

        4. Twigs glabrous; buds yellowish-gray .... **Q. velutina**

        4. Twigs tomentose or pubescent; buds reddish-brown .... **Q. marilandica**

     3. Buds not covered with dense wool, not prominently angled.

        5. Buds sharp-pointed, light chestnut-brown, glabrous or sometimes slightly hairy at the apex; bark dark brown, roughened by continuous flat-topped ridges separated by shallow fissures; acorn cups cup-shaped, with tightly appressed scales .... **Q. borealis***

---

* **Q. borealis** var. **maxima**, with larger acorns and flat saucer-shaped cup, is more common than the species in many localities in the Northern States.

5. Buds blunt or rounded, reddish-brown, glabrous or woolly above the middle, (sometimes silvery-pubescent at first); bark intermediate between *Q. velutina* and *Q. borealis;* acorn cups top-shaped to hemispheric.
....**Q. coccinea**

2. Buds small; terminal ones usually less than 4.5 mm. long.

6. Twigs smooth and glossy during the first winter; buds sharp-pointed, glabrous or silky; bark on young trunks thin, on older trunks thick and roughened by shallow fissures and scaly ridges, light to dark brown; trees; acorn cups saucer-shaped.

7. Pin-like branchlets common on the lateral branches; buds glabrous, not angular ....**Q. palustris**

7. Pin-like branchlets absent from the lateral branches.

8. Buds silky or glabrescent, somewhat angular; margin of bud-scales toothed and often ciliate ....**Q. imbricaria**

8. Buds glabrous, not angled.

9. Bud-scales chestnut-brown, their margins pale, thin and dry.
....**Q. phellos**

9. Bud-scales reddish-brown, their margins ciliate ....**Q. ellipsoidalis**

6. Twigs dull and hairy during the first winter; buds glabrous; bark gray to dark brown; acorn cups saucer-shaped or with rounded base.

10. Buds blunt, glabrous or hairy; shrubs ....**Q. ilicifolia**

10. Buds acute, puberulous; trees ....**Q. rubra**

1. Fruit maturing the first season; shell of acorn glabrous on the inner surface.
(*White Oaks*)

11. Buds narrow, pointed or blunt; terminal ones mostly 5 mm. long or more.

12. Lateral buds usually appressed; twigs yellowish-brown; branchlets often with corky ridges; bark intermediate between that of *Q. alba* and *Q. montana;* acorn cups sessile or stalked, fringed by awns of the scales.
....**Q. macrocarpa**

12. Lateral buds divergent; twigs orange to reddish-brown; branchlets without corky ridges; acorn cups not fringed by awns of the scales.

13. Twigs stout, glabrous; bark brown to black, thick, with broad continuous fissures and solid sharp-angled ridges without scales; acorn cups thin, hemispheric, with short stalks ....**Q. Prinus**

13. Twigs slender or stout, hairy or glabrous; bark thick with irregular fissures and grayish or brownish scales; acorn cups thin, shallow, cup-shaped, sessile or nearly so.

14. Bud-scales chestnut brown, with white, scarious margins.
....**Q. Muhlenbergii**

14. Bud-scales dark red, with pale margins ....**Q. Michauxii**

11. Buds broadly ovoid, rounded; the terminal 2–6 mm. long or more.

15. Buds mostly 5 mm. long or more.

16. Buds pubescent, not angular, the lateral buds appressed; twigs gray.

17. Twigs pubescent; branchlets without corky ridges; buds chestnut-brown ....**Q. stellata**

17. Twigs glabrous or puberulent; branchlets often with corky ridges; buds reddish-brown ....**Q. macrocarpa**
16. Buds glabrous or nearly so, somewhat angular, the lateral buds divergent; twigs reddish; branchlets without corky ridges; bark dark gray or brown, with irregular shallow fissures and flat ridges without scales; acorn cups hemispheric, not fringed by awns ....**Q. robur**
15. Buds mostly 2–4 mm. long.
   18. Shrubs ....**Q. prinoides**
   18. Trees.
      19. Buds reddish-brown; twigs gray to purple; bark of young branches not peeling off in scales; bark thick, light gray or white, mostly with shallow fissures and irregular flat scales or sometimes with scaly ridges; acorn cups thick, bowl-shaped, sessile or on short stalks.
      Q. alba
      19. Buds chestnut-brown; twigs light orange to reddish-brown; bark thick, brown or grayish-brown, with fissures and flat scaly ridges.
         20. Bark of young branchlets separating into curling scales; acorn cups deeply saucer-shaped on long slender stalks ....**Q. bicolor**
         20. Bark of young branches not separating into scales; acorn cups urn-shaped, sessile or short stalked ....**Q. lyrata**

Rhamnus—*Buckthorn*

1. Buds scaly.
   2. Leaves and buds opposite or sub-opposite; twigs mostly ending in sharp black spines ....**R. cathartica**
   2. Leaves and buds alternate; twigs not ending in spines.
      3. Leaves ovate; twigs glabrous, red or brown in winter; low shrub.
      R. alnifolia
      3. Leaves oblong-lanceolate; twigs often downy, gray in winter; tall shrub.
      R. lanceolata
1. Buds naked.
   4. Leaf margins serrate or serrulate; leaves glabrous on lower surface.
   R. caroliniana
   4. Leaf margins entire or undulate; leaves pubescent on lower surface.
   R. Frangula

Rhododendron—*Rhododendrons and Azaleas*

Summer Key

1. Leaves coriaceous, persistent.
   2. Leaves .5–2 cm. long; leaves and twigs dotted with rusty-brown scales; stems prostrate ....**R. lapponicum**
   2. Leaves 5–20 cm. long, not dotted with rusty-brown scales; erect shrubs or small trees.
      3. Base of leaf tapering ....**R. maximum**
      3. Base of leaf rounded ....**R. catawbiense**

1. Leaves not coriaceous, deciduous.
    4. Twigs glabrous.
        5. Leaves glabrous .... **R. arborescens**
        5. Leaves with strigose hairs, especially on midrib .... **R. canadense**
    4. Twigs not glabrous.
        6. Twigs and midrib of leaves with bristly brown hairs .... **R. viscosum**
        6. Twigs and midrib of leaves without bristly brown hairs.
            7. Leaves softly pubescent on lower surface; capsule glandular.
                    R. canescens
            7. Leaves glabrate or hairy along margin and midrib; capsule strigose.
                    R. nudiflorum

Winter Key

1. Leaves coriaceous, persistent.
    2. Leaves .5-2 cm. long; leaves and twigs dotted with rusty-brown scales;
        stems prostrate .... **R. lapponicum**
    2. Leaves 5-20 cm. long, not dotted with rusty-brown scales; erect shrubs or
        small trees.
        3. Base of leaf tapering .... **R. maximum**
        3. Base of leaf rounded .... **R. catawbiense**
1. Leaves not coriaceous, deciduous.
    4. Buds glabrous.
        5. Twigs glabrous .... **R. arborescens**
        5. Twigs with long hairs .... **R. nudiflorum**
    4. Buds puberulous.
        6. Leaf scars raised; flower buds with few early falling scales.
                    R. canadense
        6. Leaf scars not raised; flower buds with many persistent imbricated scales.
            7. Twigs tomentulose, at least at tip .... **R. canescens**
            7. Twigs glabrate, or with stalked glands or with bristly brown hairs.
                    R. viscosum and **nudiflorum**

Rhus—*Sumacs*

Summer Key

Note: *Rhus Toxicodendron, and R. Vernix are poisonous and produce a dermatitis in susceptible persons. See note on page 25.*

1. Leaves with three leaflets.
    2. Lateral buds imbedded under the base of the petioles; aerial rootlets absent;
        catkins present; fruits red, in terminal clusters; central leaflet with cuneate
        base; (crushed leaves sweet-scented) .... **R. aromatica**
    2. Lateral buds visible in the leaf axils; aerial rootlets often present; catkins
        absent; fruits axillary, whitish; central leaflet without cuneate base, long
        stalked; leaflets with variable margin .... **R. Toxicodendron**

1. Leaves with more than three leaflets.
  4. Leaflets decurrent on the rhachis; fruits red, in terminal clusters.
                                                                R. copallina
  4. Leaflets not decurrent on the rhachis.
    5. Leaflets with entire margins; fruits white, in axillary clusters....**R. Vernix**
    5. Leaflets with serrate margins; fruits red, in terminal clusters.
      6. Leaves and twigs hairy ....**R. typhina**
      6. Leaves and twigs glabrous ....**R. glabra**

Winter Key

1. Leaf-scars round; catkins present; (buds small, yellow, imbedded under the leaf-scars; twigs slender; low shrubs; fruit red) ....**R. aromatica**
1. Leaf-scars not round; catkins absent.
  2. Leaf-scars broadly crescent-shaped; fruits white, in axillary clusters.
    3. Twigs slender; buds stalked, naked; erect shrubs or climbing by aerial roots ....**R. Toxicodendron**
    3. Twigs stout; buds sessile, scaly; large erect shrubs.
      4. Twigs glabrous; lenticels inconspicuous ....**R. Vernix**
      4. Twigs puberulent or downy; lenticels prominent ....**R. copallina**
  2. Leaf-scars U-shaped, almost surrounding the buds, or C-shaped; fruit red, in terminal clusters.
    5. Twigs glabrous, three-sided ....**R. glabra**
    5. Twigs hairy, terete or nearly so.
      6. Twigs densely hairy; lenticels inconspicuous ....**R. typhina**
      6. Twigs puberulent or downy; lenticels prominent, corky, raised.
                                                                R. copallina

Ribes—*Gooseberries and Currants*

1. Stems and twigs without spines or prickles; fruits in racemes. (*Ribes hirtellum,* with black berries, solitary or in clusters of 2–4, may be without spines.)
  2. Leaves, twigs, and buds provided with scattered, sessile, yellow resin glands; berry black.
    3. Resin glands present on the upper surface of leaf; twigs glabrate; inner bark without fetid odor; leaf-scar with decurrent ridge from back.
                                                                R. americanum
    3. Resin glands absent on the upper surface of leaf; twigs puberulent; inner bark with fetid odor; leaf-scar without decurrent ridge ....**R. nigrum**
  2. Leaves, twigs, and buds without yellow resin glands.
    4. Erect bushy shrubs.
      5. Branchlets light brown, puberulent; leaves convolute in bud; berry black ....**R. odoratum**
      5. Branchlets olive-brown to gray, glabrate; leaves plicate in bud; berry red ....**R. sativum**

4. Low, prostrate or creeping shrubs; berry red.
    6. Leaves with 5–7 prominent lobes; inner bark with fetid odor; buds green or reddish-purple, fusiform; berry glandular-bristly .....**R. glandulosum**
    6. Leaves with 3–5 prominent lobes; inner bark without fetid odor; buds grayish-brown, ovate; berry glabrous ....**R. triste**
1. Stems and twigs with spines, or prickles, or both; fruits solitary or 2–5 in a cluster.
    7. Branches covered with internodal prickles nearly as long as the nodal spines.
        8. Branchlets red-brown; berries hairy, black, in racemes ....**R. lacustre**
        8. Branchlets gray or dark brownish; berries spiny, red, in clusters of 1–4.
        R. Cynosbati
    7. Branches without internodal prickles or, if present, few and shorter than the nodal spines.
        9. Berries spiny or hairy.
            10. Berry spiny, red ....**R. Cynosbati**
            10. Berry pubescent or glandular-bristly; red or green ......**R. Grossularia**
        9. Berries without spines or hairs; dark purple or black.
            11. Petiole hairs branched; lobes of leaves acute ....**R. hirtellum**
            11. Petiole hairs simple, glandular, or absent; lobes of leaves obtuse.
                12. Spines usually solitary ....**R. rotundifolium**
                12. Spines usually two or three together ....**R. gracile**

Robinia—*Locusts*

1. Twigs densely-hispid; axillary buds usually visible in winter; low shrub; legume glandular-hispid ....**R. hispida**
1. Twigs not hispid; buds usually imbedded beneath surface of leaf-scars in winter; trees.
    2. Twigs covered with sticky glandular hairs; prickles weak, base not dilated; legume glandular-hispid ....**R. viscosa**
    2. Twigs glabrous or slightly pubescent; nodal spines with dilated bases; legumes smooth ....**R. Pseudo-Acacia**

Rubus—*Raspberries, Blackberries, Dewberries* *

1. Leaves simple; palmately lobed; bark exfoliating in thin layers ....**R. odoratus**
1. Leaves compound; bark not exfoliating.
    2. Leaves glaucous-white on the lower surface, mostly 3–5 pinnate; stems terete, glaucous, or if not glaucous then erect and bristly hairy.
        3. Stems erect, somewhat glaucous when young, covered with stiff straight bristly hairs; fruit red ....**R. idaeus**
        3. Stems recurved, very glaucous; prickles recurved; fruit black or red.
            4. Stems and petioles armed with stout hooked prickles; fruit black.
            R. occidentalis
            4. Stems, petioles, and midribs armed with stout spines interspersed with slender bristles and gland-tipped hairs; fruit red ......**R. phoenicolasius**

2. Leaves not glaucous-white on the lower surface; stems not glaucous, angular or if terete then trailing.
    5. Stems trailing or prostrate, terete; pedicels with prickles.
        6. Prickles on stems stout, enlarged at base; leaves membranous, dull on upper surface; fruit black .... **R. flagellaris**
        6. Prickles on stems slender, bristly, not enlarged at base; leaves subcoriaceous, glossy on upper surface; fruit reddish-purple .... **R. hispidus**
    5. Stems erect or recurved, not trailing, angular.
        7. Leaflets laciniate-cleft .... **R. laciniatus**
        7. Leaflets not laciniate-cleft.
            8. Leaves glabrous or nearly so on both surfaces .... **R. canadensis**
            8. Leaves velvety on the lower surface and often villous or somewhat pubescent on the upper surface .... **R. allegheniensis**
   * Only a few species representing some of the more common types of *Rubus* are here included. For an exhaustive treatment see Bailey, L. H., The genus Rubus in N.A. Gentes Herbarum. 5: 1941–1945.

Salix—*Willows*

Based upon mature foliage

This key, except for a few changes, is based upon the one by Karl M. Wiegand and Arthur J. Eames in the Flora of the Cayuga Lake Basin, New York. Cornell Univ. Memoir **92**. 166–167, 1926.

1. Leaves entire, glabrous; apex obtuse or rounded .... **S. pedicellaris**
1. Leaves toothed; apex subacute or acuminate.
    2. Lower surface of leaf more or less tomentose; upper surface more or less rugose.
        3. Leaves elliptical or oblanceolate to ovate.
            4. Blade 2–3 times as long as wide, margin flat, the upper surface more or less pubescent .... **S. Bebbiana**
            4. Blade 3–4 times as long as wide, margin revolute, the upper surface glabrous or glabrate .... **S. humilis**
        3. Leaves narrowly oblanceolate to linear-lanceolate; margin revolute.
            5. Twigs 1–2 mm. in diameter; plant .5 meter or less high .... **S. tristis**
            5. Twigs 2–4 mm. in diameter; plant .5–2 meters high .... **S. candida**
    2. Lower surface of leaf glabrous or silky; upper surface not distinctly rugose.
        6. Lower surface of leaf green or only slightly paler than the upper, neither glaucous nor white-silky.
            7. Leaves linear-lanceolate to linear, blade 8–20 times as long as wide.
                8. Leaves tapering at base, sessile or nearly so; teeth distant, 2–4 per cm.; twigs tough; shrubs .... **S. interior**

8. Leaves rounded or obtuse at base, with a very short but distinct petiole; teeth close, 5–12 per cm.; twigs brittle at base; trees ....**S. nigra**

7. Leaves lanceolate to ovate; blade 2–7 times as long as wide; twigs not brittle.

  9. Leaves, especially on the sucker shoots, caudate-acuminate, lustrous.
                                                S. lucida

  9. Leaves merely acuminate.
    10. Leaves mostly 4–10 mm. wide, acute or tapering at base; stipules lacking or ephemeral ....**S. petiolaris**
    10. Leaves mostly 15–30 mm. wide, obtuse, rounded, or subcordate, rarely acute at base.
      11. Leaves firm, lustrous; teeth very fine, 10–20 per cm.; stipules early deciduous ....**S. serissima**
      11. Leaves thinner, not lustrous; teeth coarser, 3–8 per cm.; stipules usually persistent ....**S. rigida**

6. Leaves much paler on the lower surface, usually glaucous, sometimes white-silky.

  12. Blade with serrations mostly lacking on the lower third.
    13. Leaves subopposite, cuneate-oblanceolate, bluish-green; stipules early deciduous ....**S. purpurea**
    13. Leaves strictly alternate, lanceolate, elliptical or oblanceolate, not bluish-green.
      14. Leaves narrow, 4–10 mm. wide; serrations sharp, minute, 6–15 per cm.; stipules early deciduous or obsolete ....**S. petiolaris**
      14. Leaves broader, 18–50 mm. wide; serrations sub-crenate, uneven, 1–4 per cm.; stipules usually persistent ....**S. discolor**
  12. Blade serrate almost or quite to the base.
    15. Leaves long-tapering at apex, drooping; twigs slender; trees.
      16. Leaves lanceolate with rounded base; margins crenate-serrate; teeth 7–12 per cm.; petioles slender, 10–30 mm. long .....**S. amygdaloides**
      16. Leaves linear-lanceolate with acute or tapering base; margins sharply serrate; teeth coarser, 4–8 per cm.; petioles stouter, 3–10 mm. long.
                      S. babylonica and **S. blanda***
    15. Leaves acute or acuminate at apex, not long-tapering, nor drooping; twigs stouter.
      17. Serrations coarse, 3–6 per cm., .4–1 mm. high; leaves rather firm, glabrous or nearly so; twigs fragile at base; trees ....**S. fragilis**
      17. Serrations 7–12 per cm., .1–.4 mm. high; trees or shrubs.
        18. Leaves firm in texture, scarcely blackening in drying, tapering at base; trees.
          19. Leaves distinctly silky on upper surface; twigs greenish....**S. alba**

---

* S. *blanda* has less strongly pendulous twigs, broader leaves, and longer petioles than S. *babylonica.*

19. Leaves sub-glabrous on upper surface; twigs yellowish.
S. alba var. vitellina

18. Leaves thinner, tending to blacken in drying, tapering or rounded at base; veins somewhat more prominent and less regular; twigs rather stiff, ascending.
   20. Blade small, narrow, 4–10 mm. wide; pubescence when present tawny or rusty; twigs generally fascicled towards ends of branchlets.
S. petiolaris
   20. Blade usually larger and wider, 10–30 mm. wide; twigs rarely conspicuously fascicled.
      21. Leaves more or less white-silky on the lower surface .... S. sericea
      21. Leaves not silky .... S. rigida

Sambucus—*Elder*

1. Pith orange to reddish-brown; buds ovate, purplish, large ...... S. racemosa
1. Pith white; buds conical, greenish or brown, small .... S. canadensis

Shepherdia—*Buffalo-berry*

1. Leaves ovate, green above, silvery beneath; twigs brown with scurf; stems thornless .... S. canadensis
1. Leaves oblong, silvery on both surfaces; twigs silvery with scales or somewhat brownish; stems mostly thorny .... S. argentea

Smilax—*Greenbriers*

1. Leaves oblong-lanceolate to linear, tapered at base.
   2. Leaves thin, deciduous; fruit dull red .... S. lanceolata
   2. Leaves coriaceous, persistent; fruit black .... S. laurifolia
1. Leaves ovate or rounded, mostly rounded or cordate at base.
   3. Leaves glaucous on the lower surface .... S. glauca
   3. Leaves green on both surfaces.
      4. Leaves contracted above the base or three-lobed .... S. Bona-nox
      4. Leaves ovate or rounded, heart-shaped.
         5. Leaves thin; stem terete; branchlets nearly terete .... S. hispida
         5. Leaves thick; branchlets angled.
            6. Stem unarmed or somewhat prickly near the base; fruit coral-red.
S. Walteri
            6. Stem and branchlets armed with stout spines; fruit blue-black.
S. rotundifolia

Spiraea—*Spirea*

1. Stems and lower surface of leaves woolly .... S. tomentosa
1. Stems and leaves not woolly.
   2. Stems yellowish-brown; leaves finely serrate .... S. alba
   2. Stems red or purplish-brown; leaves coarsely serrate .... S. latifolia

Symphoricarpos—*Snowberry, Coralberry*

1. Pith continuous; fruits red, in dense clusters ....**S. orbiculatus**
1. Pith hollow; fruits white ....**S. albus**

Taxus—*Yew*

1. Plants low, creeping or ascending ....**T. canadensis**
1. Plants erect ....**T. cuspidata**

Ulmus—*Elms*
Summer Key

1. Leaves very scabrous on the upper surface, sometimes three-lobed at apex.
  2. Leaves ovate-oblong ....**U. rubra**
  2. Leaves obovate ....**U. glabra**
1. Leaves smooth or nearly so on the upper surface.
  3. Corky wing-like ridges usually present on twigs or branchlets.
    4. Leaves 1–3 cm. wide ....**U. alata**
    4. Leaves 4–8 cm. wide ....**U. Thomasii**
  3. Corky wing-like ridges not present on twigs or branchlets.
    5. Leaves usually 10–15 cm. long ....**U. americana**
    5. Leaves about 4–8 cm. long ....**U. campestris**

Winter Key

1. Corky wing-like ridges usually present on twigs or branchlets.
  2. Buds usually less than 5 mm. long, slender, acute ....**U. alata**
  2. Buds 6–8 mm. long ....**U. Thomasii**
1. Corky wing-like ridges not present on twigs and branchlets.
  3. Buds densely rusty-brown hairy; twigs gray-buff, rough; inner bark muci-
    laginous ....**U. rubra**
  3. Buds not densely rusty-brown hairy; twigs red-brown or grayish-brown,
    smooth or hairy.
    4. Buds chestnut-brown; bud-scales with darker margins; bark of trunk
      ridged, inner bark not mucilaginous.
      5. Tree excurrent, with a cylindrical crown; buds usually divergent.
        U. Thomasii
      5. Tree deliquescent with a broad vase-shaped crown; buds somewhat
        appressed ....**U. americana**
    4. Buds smoky-brown or almost black; bud-scales uniformly dark through-
      out.
      6. Twigs hispid; bark of trunk light, smooth or with broad flat-topped
        longitudinal ridges; inner bark somewhat mucilaginous; trunk deli-
        quescent, with several erect branches forming a round-topped crown.
        U. glabra

6. Twigs glabrescent; bark of trunk dark, rough, the ridges breaking into oblong blocks, inner bark not mucilaginous; trunk of tree somewhat continuous but forming a spreading crown ....**U. campestris**

Vaccinium—*Blueberries and Cranberries*

1. Leaves persistent; stems creeping or trailing; berry red.
  2. Leaves with dark bristly points on the lower surface; stems somewhat tufted ....**V. Vitis-Idaea**
  2. Leaves without dark points, glaucous-white on the lower surface; stems very slender.
    3. Leaves strongly revolute, narrowly ovate, pointed at apex, 4–8 mm. long.
      V. Oxycoccus
    3. Leaves flat or slightly revolute, elliptical, blunt or rounded at apex, 10–18 mm. long ....**V. macrocarpon**
1. Leaves deciduous; stems usually erect.
  4. Stems from 2–20 dm. high.
    5. Leaves glaucous or very pale on the lower surface, margin of leaves usually entire or only minutely serrulate.
      6. Branchlets ascending, glabrous, usually green, covered with speckles; berry blue ....**V. vacillans**
      6. Branchlets recurved–spreading, hairy, not covered with speckles; berry greenish-yellow ....**V. stamineum**
    5. Leaves bright green on the lower surface, or margin not entire; berry blue.
      7. Margin of leaves entire.
        8. Leaves mostly 2–4 cm. long; leaves and twigs very hairy; bark of branchlets covered with speckles ....**V. myrtilloides**
        8. Leaves mostly .5–2 cm. long; leaves and twigs glabrous or nearly so; bark of branchlets shredding ....**V. uliginosum**
      7. Margin of leaves serrate or serrulate.
        9. Leaves lanceolate, serrulate; branchlets grooved ....**V. angustifolium**
        9. Leaves obovate or spatulate, crenulate-serrulate; branchlets round.
          V. caespitosum
  4. Stems 1–10 meters high.
    10. Leaves ovate to elliptic-lanceolate, entire or serrulate, dull; branchlets green to red, speckled; tall shrubs.
      V. corymbosum and several related forms.
    10. Leaves obovate to oblong or orbicular, denticulate or entire, glossy; branchlets red-brown; small trees ....**V. arboreum**

Viburnum—*Arrow-woods, etc.*

Summer Key

1. Leaves lobed, palmately veined.
  2. Glands present on the petioles; stipules present; drupe red.
    3. Leaves pubescent on the lower surface.....................**V. Opulus**
    3. Leaves glabrous except along the veins ......**V. Opulus** var. **americanum**
  2. Glands absent from the petioles.

4. Stipules present; leaves densely pubescent on lower surface; glands absent on blade; drupe purple-black . . . .**V. acerifolium**

4. Stipules absent; leaves glabrate; glands present on the lower teeth of the blade; drupe red . . . .**V. pauciflorum**

1. Leaves not lobed, pinnately veined.

5. Buds naked.

6. Lower surface of leaves, twigs, and buds covered with a gray stellate pubescence; drupe red changing to almost black . . . .**V. Lantana**

6. Lower surface of leaves and twigs very rusty-scurfy; drupe red.
   V. alnifolium

5. Buds scaly.

7. Margin of leaves coarsely toothed, secondary veins extending to the teeth; outer pair of bud-scales shorter than the bud.

8. Stipules present.

9. Older bark close, not exfoliating; petioles often shorter than the stipules . . . .**V. Rafinesquianum**

9. Older bark exfoliating in thin flakes; petioles longer than the stipules.
   V. molle

8. Stipules absent.

10. Petioles glabrous; lower surface of leaves glabrous or with simple hairs . . . .**V. dentatum**

10. Petioles and lower surface of leaves stellate-tomentose.

11. Marginal teeth acute . . . .**V. pubescens**

11. Marginal teeth blunt . . . .**V. scabrellum**

7. Margin of leaves entire or finely and closely toothed; secondary veins not extending to the leaf margin; outer pair of bud-scales as long as the bud, valvate; (twigs and buds usually scurfy).

12. Cymes peduncled; leaf margin entire or somewhat wavy-toothed.

13. Leaves glossy above, margin usually entire; peduncle as long as or longer than the cyme . . . .**V. nudum**

13. Leaves dull above, margin usually wavy-toothed; peduncle shorter than the cyme . . . .**V. cassinoides**

12. Cymes sessile; leaf margin finely or sharply toothed.

14. Margin of petiole narrow, not wavy, or absent; lower surface of leaves not brown-tomentose; leaves acute or rounded at apex.
    V. prunifolium

14. Margin of petiole broad and wavy.

15. Lower surface of leaves rusty-tomentose. . . . .**V. rufidulum**

15. Lower surface of leaves not rusty-tomentose; leaves acuminate.
    V. Lentago

Winter Key

1. Buds naked, densely tomentose.

2. Buds light cinnamon-brown; leaf-scars mostly 2–5 mm. wide; twigs glossy purplish-brown . . . .**V. alnifolium**

    2. Buds brownish-gray; leaf-scars mostly 1 mm. wide; twigs dull, usually brown ....**V. Lantana**

1. Buds scaly, rarely tomentose but sometimes pubescent.
   3. Outer pair of bud-scales shorter than the bud.
      4. Bark of stem and branches exfoliating ....**V. molle**
      4. Bark of stem and branches not exfoliating.
         5. Twigs without longitudinal ridges.
            6. Twigs glabrous; lateral buds plump and spreading.
                                       V. Rafinesquianum
            6. Twigs hairy; lateral buds elongated and appressed ....**V. acerifolium**
         5. Twigs with longitudinal ridges.
            7. Twigs and buds glabrous, smooth; branchlets gray; buds slender and appressed ....**V. dentatum**
            7. Twigs and buds hairy, rough; buds divergent.
               8. Branchlets reddish-brown ....**V. scabrellum**
               8. Branchlets gray-brown ....**V. pubescens**
   3. Outer pair of bud-scales as long as the bud, valvate.
      9. Buds glabrous or glutinous, not scurfy, oblong or ovoid, with rounded apex.
         10. Stems tall, erect ....**V. Opulus** and var. **americanum**
         10. Stems low, straggling ....**V. pauciflorum**
      9. Buds scurfy or hairy, linear-lanceolate; flower buds swollen at base.
         11. Buds very red-tomentose ....**V. rufidulum**
         11. Buds gray or reddish-brown, scurfy or pubescent.
            12. Twigs mostly short and stiff, nearly at right angles to the stem; buds mostly short-pointed, often rusty-pubescent or scurfy.
                                     V. prunifolium
            12. Twigs mostly long and flexuous, ascending; buds long-pointed, scurfy, reddish-brown or lead-colored.
               13. Bud-scales thin, broadened at the base; flower-buds, before swelling, completely covered by the outer pair of bud-scales.
                                      V. Lentago
               13. Bud-scales thick, not broadened at the base; flower-buds, before swelling, not completely covered by outer pair of bud-scales.
                  14. Peduncle shorter than the cyme.................**V. cassinoides**
                  14. Peduncle as long as or longer than the cyme ....**V. nudum**

Vitis—*Grape*

1. A tendril (or inflorescence) opposite each of several successive leaves, twigs and lower surface of leaves rusty-woolly ....**V. Labrusca**
1. Tendrils intermittent, none opposite each third leaf.
    2. Leaves pubescent and floccose, especially on the lower surface and when young.
      3. Branchlets angular; leaves at first pubescent, later pale gray-green.
                                         V. cinerea
      3. Branchlets terete.

4. Lower surface of leaves rusty-brown with floccose hairs; petiole pubescent.
   V. aestivalis

4. Lower surface of leaves glaucous and often becoming glabrate; petiole nearly glabrous, often glaucous and red ....**V. argentifolia***

2. Leaves glabrous and mostly glossy (often short hairy on the lower surface, especially on the veins) ....**V. riparia**

* *Vitis argentifolia,* according to L. H. Bailey, is the common northern grape which has usually been referred to as *V. bicolor* or *V. aestivalis* var. *bicolor* by many American authors. For a more detailed description of these and other American grapes see L. H. Bailey, Gentes Herbarum 3:151–244. 1934; and also M. L. Fernald, Rhodora 41:431–434. 1939.

Zanthoxylum—*Prickly Ash, Toothache-tree*

1. Base of leaflets often oblique; fruits in terminal cyme; buds dark-brown or nearly black ....**Z. Clava-Herculis**

1. Base of leaflets not oblique; fruits in axillary clusters; buds red.
   Z. americanum

Pyrus—*Apples, Pears, Mountain Ashes, and Chokeberries*

1. Leaves pinnately compound. (*Sorbus*).
   2. Outer bud-scales woolly, not gummy; apex of leaves usually blunt or rounded, fruit about 10 mm. in diameter ....**P. Aucuparia**
   2. Outer bud-scales glabrous and gummy; apex of leaves usually acute.
      3. Fruits 4–6 mm. in diameter ....**P. americana**
      3. Fruits 8–10 mm. in diameter ....**P. decora**
1. Leaves simple.
   4. Midrib of leaf with dark glands on the upper surface; fruit mostly less than 1 cm. in diameter, berry-like. (*Aronia*).
      5. · Twigs, buds and leaves glabrous or glabrate; fruit dark purple or black.
         P. melanocarpa
      5. Twigs, buds and lower surface of leaves canescent-tomentose.
         6. Fruits red ....**P. arbutifolia**
         6. Fruits purplish-black ....**P. arbutifolia var. atropurpurea**
   4. Midrib of leaf without dark glands on the upper surface; fruit large, 3–10 cm. in diameter, or larger.
      7. Crown of tree narrow; buds and surface of leaves glabrous or glabrate.
         P. communis
      7. Crown of tree low and spreading; buds and lower surface of leaves usually woolly.
         8. Mature leaves soft-pubescent or tomentose on the lower surface; buds blunt, tomentose or pubescent; branches rarely thorny ....**P. Malus**
         8. Mature leaves glabrous or nearly so; buds long and narrow, glabrous; branches usually thorny ....**P. coronaria**

C. A SYSTEMATIC LIST OF THE SPECIES INCLUDED IN THE KEYS

Species preceded by a letter are introduced in the Northeastern United States; all others are native. A = native of Asia; E = native of Europe; W = native of Western N. A.; S = native of Southern U. S.; a period after the letter preceding an introduced species indicates that it has become naturalized, at least to some extent, in the Northeastern U. S.; a letter without a period indicates that the species is found only in cultivation.

GYMNOSPERMAE

GINKGOALES
1. Ginkgoaceae
A   Ginkgo biloba L. (*Salisburia adiantifolia* Smith) Ginkgo, Maidenhair Tree

CONIFERALES
2. Taxaceae
Taxus canadensis Marsh. (*T. minor* Britt.) American Yew, Ground Hemlock
A   Taxus cuspidata Sieb. and Zucc. Japanese Yew

3. Pinaceae
Pinus Banksiana Lamb. (*P. divaricata* Du Mont de Cours.) Jack Pine, Gray Pine
E   Pinus cembra L. Swiss Stone Pine
W   Pinus contorta var. latifolia S. Wats. (*P. contorta* var. *Murrayana* Engelm.) Lodgepole Pine
Pinus echinata Mill. (*P. mitis* Michx.) Yellow Pine, Shortleaf Pine
A   Pinus Griffithsii McClelland (*P. excelsa* Wall.) Himalayan Pine
E   Pinus Mugo var. Mughus Zenari. (*P. montana* var. *Mughus* Willk.) Swiss Mountain Pine
W   Pinus monticola Lamb. Western White Pine
E   Pinus nigra Arnold var. austriaca Aschers. and Graebn. (*P. Laricio* var. *austriaca* Endl.) Austrian Pine
Pinus palustris Mill. Long-leaved Pine
Pinus pungens Lamb. Table Mountain Pine, Hickory Pine
W   Pinus ponderosa Laws. Western Yellow Pine, Bull Pine. (Also native westward.)
Pinus resinosa Ait. Red Pine, Norway Pine
Pinus rigida Mill. Pitch Pine
Pinus strobus L. White Pine
E   Pinus sylvestris L. Scotch Pine
Pinus taeda L. Loblolly Pine, Old Field Pine
Pinus virginiana Mill. (*P. inops* Ait.) Jersey Pine, Scrub Pine
E   Larix decidua Mill. (*L. europaea* DC.) European Larch
Larix laricina (Du Roi) Koch. (*L. americana* Michx.) Tamarack, Larch
E   Picea Abies (L.) Karst. (*P. excelsa* Link.) Norway Spruce
Picea glauca (Moench.) Voss. (*P. canadensis* BSP.) White Spruce, Skunk or Cat Spruce
Picea mariana (Mill.) BSP. Black Spruce, Swamp Spruce
W   Picea pungens Engelm. (*P. parryana* Sarg.) Colorado Spruce, Blue Spruce
Picea rubens Sarg. (*P. rubra* (Dur.) Link) Red Spruce
Abies balsamea (L.) Mill. Balsam Fir, Balsam
W   Abies concolor (Gord.) Engelm. White Fir, Silver Fir
Tsuga canadensis (L.) Carr. Hemlock, Hemlock Spruce
W   Pseudotsuga taxifolia (Poir.) Britt. (*P. douglasii* Carr.), (*P. mucronata* Sudw.) Douglas Fir, Douglas Spruce, Red Fir

4. Taxodiaceae
A   Sciadopitys verticillata (Thunb.) Sieb & Zucc. Umbrella-Pine
Taxodium distichum (L.) Rich. (*Cupressus disticha* L.) Bald Cypress

5. Cupressaceae
W   Chamaecyparis nootkatensis (Lamb.) Spach. (*Cupressus nootkatensis* Lamb.) Alaska Cedar, Yellow Cypress, Nootka Cypress

A   Chamaecyparis obtusa Sieb. and Zucc. (*Cupressus obtusa* Koch) Hinoki Cypress
A   Chamaecyparis pisifera Sieb. and Zucc. (*Cupressus pisifera* Koch) Sawara Cypress
    Chamaecyparis thyoides (L.) BSP. (*C. sphaeroidea* Spach) White Cedar
    Thuja occidentalis L. Arbor-vitae
A   Thuja orientalis L. (*Biota orientalis* Endl.) Oriental Arbor-vitae
W Thuja plicata D. Don. (*T. gigantea* Nutt.) Giant Arbor-vitae, Western Red Cedar
A   Thuja Standishii Carr. (*T. japonica* Maxim.) Standish Arbor-vitae
    Juniperus communis L. Common Juniper
    Juniperus communis L. var. depressa Pursh. (*J. communis* var. *canadensis* Loud.)
      Prostrate Juniper
    Juniperus horizontalis Moench. (*J. Sabina* var. *procumbens* Pursh.) Creeping Juniper
    Juniperus virginiana L. Red Cedar, Savin
W Libocedrus decurrens Torr. (*Heyderia decurrens* Koch) Incense Cedar

ANGIOSPERMAE—MONOCOTYLEDONS

LILIALES

6. Liliaceae

Smilax Bona-nox L. (*S. pseudo-china* A.DC. not L.) Halberd-leaved Smilax
Smilax glauca Walt. Saw Brier, Greenbrier
Smilax hispida Muhl. Greenbrier
Smilax lanceolata L. Greenbrier
Smilax laurifolia L. Laurel Greenbrier
Smilax rotundifolia L. Common Greenbrier, Horsebrier
Smilax Walteri Pursh. Coral Greenbrier

ANGIOSPERMAE—DICOTYLEDONS

SALICALES

7. Salicaceae

E   Salix alba L. White Willow
E. Salix alba L. var. vitellina (L.) Stokes. Golden Willow
    Salix amygdaloides Anders. Peach-leaved Willow
E. Salix babylonica L. Weeping Willow
    Salix Bebbiana Sarg. (*S. rostrata* of some authors)
    Salix blanda Anders. Wisconsin Weeping Willow. (Introduced hybrid.)
    Salix candida Fluegge. Hoary Willow
    Salix discolor Muhl. Pussy Willow
E. Salix fragilis L. Crack Willow
    Salix humilis Marsh. Prairie Willow
    Salix interior Rowlee (*S. longifolia* Muhl.)
    Salix lucida Muhl. Shining Willow
    Salix nigra Marsh. Black Willow
    Salix pedicellaris Pursh
    Salix petiolaris Smith
E. Salix purpurea L. Purple or Basket Willow
    Salix rigida Muhl. (*S. cordata* Muhl.)
    Salix sericea Marsh. Silky Willow
    Selix serissima (Bailey) Fernald. Autumn Willow
    Salix tristis Ait. Dwarf Gray Willow
E   Populus alba L. White Poplar, Silver-leaved Poplar, Abele
A. Populus candicans Ait. (*P. balsamifera* L. var. *candicans* Gray) Balm of Gilead
    Populus deltoides Marsh. (*P. monolifera* of authors) Cottonwood
    Populus grandidentata Michx. Large-toothed Aspen, Poplar
    Populus heterophylla L. Swamp Cottonwood, Downy Poplar

E Populus nigra L. var. italica Muenchh. (*P. nigra* var. *pyramidalis* Spach) Lombardy
     Poplar
     Populus tacamahaca Mill. (*P. balsamifera* of most authors) Balsam Poplar, Tacamahac
     Populus tremuloides Michx. Quaking Aspen, Aspen

MYRICALES
8. Myricaceae

Myrica cerifera L. (*Morella cerifera* (L.) Small.) Wax Myrtle
Myrica Gale L. Sweet Gale
Myrica pennsylvanica Lois. (*M. carolinensis* Amer. Authors, not Mill.) Bayberry
Myrica peregrina (L.) Ktze. (*M. asplenifolia* L., *Comptonia peregrina* (L.) Coult.)
    Sweet Fern

9. Leitneriaceae

Leitneria floridana Chapm. Cork Wood

JUGLANDALES
10. Juglandaceae

Juglans cinerea L. Butternut, White Walnut
Juglans nigra L. Black Walnut
A Juglans regia L. Persian Walnut, English Walnut
A Juglans Sieboldiana Maxim. (*J. ailantifolia* Carr.) Japanese Walnut.
     Carya Nutt. (*Hicoria* Raf.)
     Carya cordiformis (Wang.) Koch. (*C. amara* Nutt.) Bitternut, Swamp Hickory
     Carya glabra (Mill.) Sweet. (*C. porcina* Nutt.) Pignut
     Carya pecan (Marsh.) Engl. and Graebn. (*C. illinoensis* (Wang.) Koch, *C. olivaeformis*
         Nutt.) Pecan
     Carya laciniosa (Michx. f.) Loud. (*C. sulcata* Nutt.) King Nut
     Carya ovalis (Wang.) Sarg. (*C. microcarpa* Nutt.) Small Pignut
     Carya ovata (Mill.) Koch (*C. alba* Nutt.) Shagbark Hickory, Shellbark Hickory
     Carya pallida Ashe. Pale Hickory
     Carya tomentosa (Lam.) Nutt. (*C. alba* K. Koch, not Nutt.) Mocker Nut

FAGALES
11. Corylaceae (*Betulaceae*)

Corylus americana Walt. American Hazelnut
Corylus cornuta Marsh. (*C. rostrata* Ait.) Beaked Hazelnut
Ostrya virginiana (Mill.) Koch. (*O. virginica* Willd.) Hop Hornbeam, Ironwood
Carpinus caroliniana Walt. Blue Beech or American Hornbeam
Betula lenta L. Black or Cherry Birch
Betula lutea Michx. Yellow Birch
Betula nigra L. River or Red Birch
E. Betula pendula Roth. European Birch
      Betula populifolia Marsh. Gray, Old Field, or Wire Birch
      Betula papyrifera Marsh. Paper, Canoe, or White Birch
      Betula pumila L. Low or Swamp Birch
      Betula glandulosa Michx. Dwarf or Glandular Birch
      Alnus crispa (Ait.) Pursh. Green or Mountain Alder
      Alnus crispa (Ait.) Pursh. var. mollis Fernald. Downy Green Alder
E. Alnus glutinosa (L.) Gaertn. (*A. vulgaris* Hill) European Black Alder
      Alnus incana (L.) Moench. Speckled or Hoary Alder
      Alnus maritima (Marsh) Nutt. Sea-side Alder
      Alnus serrulata Willd. (*A. rugosa* (Duroi) Spreng.) Smooth or Hazel Alder

12. Fagaceae

S Fagus grandifolia Ehrh. (*F. americana* Sweet, *F. ferruginea* Ait.) Beech
     Castanea dentata (Marsh.) Borkh. Chestnut
     Castanea pumila (L.) Mill. Chinquapin
     Quercus alba L. White Oak
     Quercus bicolor Willd. (*Q. platanoides* Sudw.) Swamp White Oak
     Quercus borealis Michx. f. var. maxima (Marsh.) Ashe (*Q. rubra* Du Roi) Red Oak
     Quercus coccinea Muenchh. Scarlet Oak

Quercus ellipsoidalis E. J. Hill. Northern Pin Oak
Quercus ilicifolia Wang. (*Q. nana* Sarg.) Bear or Black Scrub Oak
Quercus imbricaria Michx. Shingle Oak or Laurel Oak
Quercus lyrata Walt. Overcup Oak
Quercus macrocarpa Michx. Bur Oak, Mossy Cup Oak
Quercus marilandica Muenchh. Black Jack or Barren Oak
Quercus Michauxii Nutt. (*Q. Prinus* L.) Basket or Cow Oak
Quercus Muhlenbergii Engelm. (*Q. acuminata* Sarg.) Yellow or Chestnut Oak
Quercus palustris Muenchh. Pin Oak
Quercus phellos L. Willow Oak
Quercus prinoides Willd. Scrub or Dwarf Chinquapin Oak
Quercus Prinus Engelm. (*Q. montana* Willd.) Chestnut or Rock Oak
EA Quercus robur L. (*Q. pedunculata* Ehrh.) English Oak
Quercus stellata Wang. (*Q. minor* Sarg.) Post Oak
Quercus rubra L. (*Q. falcata* Michx., *Q. digitata* Sudw.) Spanish Oak, Southern Red Oak
Quercus velutina Lam. (*Q. tinctoria* Bartram) Black Oak

URTICALES
13. Ulmaceae

Planera aquatica Gmel. Water Elm
Ulmus alata Michx. Wahoo, Winged Elm
Ulmus americana L. American Elm, White Elm
E. Ulmus campestris L. (*U. procera* Salisb.) English Elm
Ulmus rubra Muhl. (*U. fulva* Michx.) Slippery Elm
EA Ulmus glabra Huds. (*U. scabra* Mill., *U. montana* With.) Scotch Elm, Witch Elm
Ulmus Thomasii Sarg. (*U. racemosa* Thomas.) Cork or Rock Elm
Celtis occidentalis L. Hackberry
Celtis laevigata Willd. Sugarberry

14. Moraceae

A Broussonetia papyrifera (L.) Vent. (*Papyrius papyrifera* (L.) Ktze.) Paper Mulberry
A Ficus carica L. Common Fig
S. Maclura pomifera (Raf.) Schneid. (*Toxylon pomiferum* Raf., *M. aurantiaca* Nutt.) Osage Orange
EA. Morus alba L. White Mulberry
Morus rubra L. Red Mulberry

ARISTOLOCHIALES
15. Aristolochiaceae

Aristolochia durior Hill. (*A. Sipho* L'Her., *A. macrophylla* Lam.) Dutchman's Pipe
Aristolochia tomentosa Sims. Woolly Pipe-vine

RANALES
16. Ranunculaceae

Clematis verticillaris DC. (*Atragene americana* Sims.) Purple Clematis, Rock Clematis
Clematis virginiana L. Virgin's Bower.
Zanthorhiza apiifolia L'Her. (*Xanthorrhiza simplicissima* Marsh.) Shrub Yellow-root

17. Berberidaceae

A Berberis Thunbergii DC. Japanese Barberry
E. Berberis vulgaris L. Common Barberry
W Berberis Aquifolium Pursh. (*Mahonia Aquifolium* Nutt.) Oregon Grape or Holly

18. Menispermaceae

Calycocarpum Lyoni (Pursh) Nutt. Cupseed
Cocculus carolinus (L.) DC. Carolina Moonseed
Menispermum canadense L. Moonseed

19. Magnoliaceae

Magnolia acuminata L. Cucumber Tree, Mountain Magnolia
Magnolia Fraseri Walt. Long-leaved Cucumber Tree
S   Magnolia grandiflora L. (*M. foetida* Sarg.) Magnolia
Magnolia macrophylla Michx. Large-leaved Cucumber Tree
Magnolia tripetala L. Umbrella Tree, Elkwood
Magnolia virginiana L. (*M. glauca* L.) Sweet Bay, Swamp Bay
Liriodendron Tulipifera L. Tulip Tree, Yellow Poplar

20. Calycanthaceae

Calycanthus fertilis Walt. (*C. glaucus* and *C. laevigatus* Willd.) Butneria
S   Calycanthus floridus L. Carolina Allspice

21. Anonaceae

Asimina triloba Dunal. Papaw, Custard Apple

22. Lauraceae

Sassafras albidum (Nutt.) Nees. (*S. officinale* Nees. and Eberm.) Sassafras
Lindera Benzoin (L.) Blume (*Benzoin aestivale* (L.) Nees.) Spicebush
Lindera melissaefolium (Walt.) Nees. (*Benzoin melissaefolium* (Walt.) Nees.) Hairy
    Spicebush

ROSALES
23. Saxifragaceae

EA. Philadelphus grandiflorus Willd. Syringa or Mock Orange
S   Philadelphus pubescens Loisel. (*P. latifolius* Schrad.) Syringa or Mock Orange
S   Decumaria barbara L. Decumaria
Hydrangea arborescens L. Wild or Smooth Hydrangea
S   Hydrangea cinerea Small. Ashy Hydrangea
A   Hydrangea paniculata Sieb. var. grandiflora Sieb. Hydrangea
Itea virginica L. Sweet Spire
Ribes americanum Mill. (*R. floridum* L'Her.) Wild Black Currant
Ribes Cynosbati L. (*Grossularia Cynosbati* (L.) Mill.) Wild Gooseberry, Dogberry
Ribes glandulosum Grauer (*R. prostratum* L'Her.) Skunk or Fetid Currant
Ribes gracile Pursh. (*R. missouriensis* Nutt., *Grossularia missouriensis* Cov. and Britt.)
    Missouri Gooseberry
E. Ribes Grossularia L. (*Grossularia reclinata* Mill.) European or Garden Gooseberry
Ribes hirtelium Michx. (*R. oxycanthoides* L., *Grossularia hirtella* Spach) Smooth
    Gooseberry
Ribes lacustre (Pers.) Poir. Swamp Black Currant
E. Ribes nigrum L. European Black Currant
Ribes odoratum Wendl. (*R. aureum* Authors not Pursh) Golden or Buffalo Currant
Ribes rotundifolium Michx. (*Grossularia rotundifolia* Cov. and Britt.)
E. Ribes sativum Syme. (*R. vulgare* Authors) Garden Red Currant
Ribes triste Pall. Swamp Red Currant

24. Hamamelidaceae

Hamamelis virginiana L. Witch-hazel
Liquidambar styraciflua L. Red or Sweet Gum

25. Platanaceae

E   Platanus acerifolia Willd. London Plane (a hybrid of the next two)
Platanus occidentalis L. Sycamore or Buttonball
A   Platanus orientalis L. Oriental Plane

26. Rosaceae

Physocarpus opulifolius (L.) Maxim. Ninebark
Spiraea alba Du Roi. (*S. salicifolia* var. *paniculata* Ait.) Meadow Sweet

Spiraea latifolia (Ait.) Borkh. (*S. salicifolia* var. *latifolia* Ait.) Meadow Sweet
Spiraea tomentosa L. Hardhack or Steeplebush
A. Sorbaria sorbifolia (L). A. Braun. (*Spiraea sorbifolia* L.) Ural False-Spirea
A. Cydonia oblonga Mill. (*C. vulgaris* Pers., *Pyrus Cydonia* L.) Quince
A. Chaenomeles lagenaria (Loisel.) Koidz. Japanese Quince
Pyrus americana DC. (*Sorbus americana* Marsh.) American Mountain Ash
Pyrus arbutifolia (L.) Ell. (*Aronia arbutifolia*) Red Chokeberry
Pyrus arbutifolia var. atropurpurea Robinson (*Aronia arbutifolia* Spach var. *atropurpurea* Britt.) Purple Chokeberry.
E.A. Pyrus Aucuparia Ehrh. (*Sorbus Aucuparia* L.) European Mountain Ash or Rowan
E. Pyrus communis L. Pear
Pyrus coronaria L. (*Malus coronaria* (L.) Mill.) Wild Crab
Pyrus decora (Sarg.) Hyland. (*Sorbus dumosa*) Mountain Ash
E.A. Pyrus Malus L. (*Malus pumila* Mill.) Apple
Pyrus melanocarpa (Michx.) Willd. (*Aronia melanocarpa* Spach) Black Chokeberry
Amelanchier amabilis Wiegand. (*A. grandiflora* Wiegand.) Large-flowered Juneberry
Amelanchier arborea (Michx. f.) Fern. (*A. canadensis* Amer. authors.) Serviceberry
Amelanchier Bartramiana (Tausch.) Roem.
Amelanchier canadensis (L.) Medic. (*A. oblongifolia* (T. and G.) Roem.) Serviceberry, Juneberry
Amelanchier humilis Wiegand. (*A. spicata* Amer. authors in part) Dwarf Juneberry
Amelanchier intermedia Spach. (*A. canadensis* var. *oblongifolia* T. and G.) Swamp Shad-bush
Amelanchier laevis Wiegand. (*A. canadensis* Authors)
Amelanchier sanguinea (Pursh) DC. Round-leaved Juneberry
Amelanchier stolonifera Wiegand. (*A. spicata* Amer. authors in part)
Crataegus beata Sarg. Hawthorn
Crataegus Brainerdi Sarg.
Crataegus Calpodendron (Ehrh.) Medic.
Crataegus chrysocarpa Ashe
Crataegus coccinea L.
Crataegus Crus-galli L.
Crataegus Dodgei Ashe (*C. Margaretta*)
Crataegus filipes Ashe
Crataegus Holmesiana Ashe
Crataegus intricata Lange
Crataegus macracantha Lodd.
Crataegus macrosperma Ashe
Crataegus Margaretta Ashe
Crataegus mollis (T. and G.) Scheele
E. Crataegus monogyna Jacq. (*C. oxyacantha* of Gray's Manual) English Hawthorn
E Crataegus oxyacantha L. English Hawthorn
Crataegus pruinosa (Wendl.) C. Koch
Crataegus punctata Jacq.
Crataegus submollis Sarg.
Crataegus succulenta Schrad.
A Rhodotypos kerrioides Sieb. and Zucc. Jetbead
A Kerria japonica DC. Kerria
Potentilla fruticosa L. (*Dasiphora fruticosa* (L.) Rydb.) Shrubby Cinquefoil
Rubus allegheniensis Porter. Blackberry
Rubus canadensis L. Blackberry
Rubus flagellaris Willd. (*R. procumbens, R. villosus* of Authors) Dewberry
Rubus hispidus L. Blackberry
Rubus idaeus L. Red Raspberry
A. Rubus laciniatus Willd. Evergreen Blackberry
Rubus occidentalis L. Black Cap, Black Raspberry
Rubus odoratus L. Flowering Raspberry
E. Rubus phoenicolasius Maxim. Wineberry

EA. Rosa blanda Ait. Smooth Rose
Rosa carolina L. (*R. humilis* Marsh.) Dwarf Rose
Rosa nitida Willd.
Rosa palustris Marsh. (*R. carolina* of Gray's Manual) Swamp Rose
E Rosa rugosa Thunb.
Rosa setigera Michx. Prairie Rose
Rosa virginiana Mill.
E. Rosa Eglanteria L. (*R. rubiginosa* L.) Eglantine, Sweetbriar
Prunus americana Marsh. American Plum
EA. Prunus avium L. Sweet Cherry, Mazzard
EA Prunus Cerasus L. Sour Cherry, Morello
A. Prunus domestica L. Garden Plum
Prunus maritima Wang. Beach or Sand Plum
Prunus nigra Ait. Wild or Canada Plum
Prunus pennsylvanica L.f. Pin or Fire Cherry
A Prunus Persica Sieb. and Zucc. (*Amygdalus Persica* L.) Peach
Prunus serotina Ehrh. Wild Black Cherry
Prunus pumila L.
Prunus virginiana L. Choke Cherry

27. Leguminosae

A Caragana arborescens Lam. Pea-Tree
Gymnocladus dioica (L.) Koch. (*G. canadensis* Lam.) Kentucky Coffee Tree
Gleditsia aquatica Marsh. Water Locust
Gleditsia triacanthos L. Honey Locust
Cercis canadensis L. Redbud or Judas Tree
S Cladrastis lutea (Michx.) Koch. (*Virgilia lutea* Michx.) Yellow Wood
A Sophora japonica L. (*Styphnolobium japonicum* Schott) Japanese Pagoda Tree
E. Cytisus scoparius (L.) Link (*Spartium scoparium* L.) Scotch Broom
E Laburnum anagyroides Medic. (*L. vulgare* Griseb.) Golden Chain
Amorpha fruticosa L. (*A. fragrans* Sweet) False or Bastard Indigo
S. Robinia hispida L. Rose Acacia
Robinia Pseudo-acacia L. Common or Black Locust
S Robinia viscosa Vent. Clammy Locust
A Wisteria sinensis Sweet. (*W. chinensis* DC., *Kraunhia sinensis* Makino.) Chinese
Wisteria

GERANIALES
28. Rutaceae

A Citrus trifoliata L. (*Poncirus trifoliata* Raf.) Trifoliate Orange
Zanthoxylum americanum Mill. Prickly Ash
Zanthoxylum Clava-Herculis L. (*Z. carolinianum* Lam., *Fagara Clava-Herculis*
Small.) Toothache-tree or Hercules-club
Ptelea trifoliata L. Hop Tree or Wafer Ash

29. Simarubaceae

A. Ailanthus altissima (Mill.) Swingle. (*A. glandulosa* Desf.) Ailanthus, Tree of Heaven

SAPINDALES
30. Buxaceae

EA Buxus sempervirens L. Common Box

31. Empetraceae

Empetrum nigrum L. Crowberry
Corema Conradii (Torr.) Loud. Conrad's Crowberry

32. Anacardiaceae

Rhus aromatica Ait. (*R. canadensis* Marsh.) Aromatic or Fragrant Sumac
Rhus copallina L. Dwarf or Shining Sumac.
Rhus glabra L. Smooth Sumac
Rhus Toxicodendron L. (*R. radicans* L., *Toxicodendron radicans* (L.) Ktze.) Poison
    Ivy, Poison Oak. See note on page 25.
Rhus typhina L. (*R. hirta* Sudw.) Staghorn Sumac
Rhus Vernix L. (*Toxicodendron Vernix* (L.) Ktze.) Poison or Swamp Sumac
EA Cotinus Coggyria Scop. (*Rhus Cotinus* L.) Smoke-tree

33. Aquifoliaceae

Ilex decidua Walt. Deciduous Holly, Possum-haw
Ilex glabra (L.) A. Gray. Inkberry
Ilex laevigata (Dum.-Cours) Gray. Smooth Winterberry
Ilex montana Gray. (*I. monticola* A. Gray) Large-leaved Holly
Ilex opaca Ait. American Holly
Ilex verticillata (L.) Gray. Winterberry or Black Alder
Nemopanthus mucronata (L.) Trelease (*N. fascicularis* Raf.) Mountain Holly

34. Celastraceae

A Evonymus alata Maxim.
Evonymus americana L. Strawberry Bush
Evonymus atropurpurea Jacq. Burning Bush or Wahoo
E Evonymus europaea L. Spindle Tree
Evonymus obovata Nutt. (*E. americanus* var. *obovatus* T. and G.) Running Straw-
    berry Bush
A Evonymus Fortunei (Turcz.) Hand. Mazz. (*E. radicans* Sieb.) Wintercreeper
Pachistima Canbyi Gray. Canby Pachistima
Celastrus scandens L. American Bittersweet, Waxwork

35. Staphyleaceae

Staphylea trifolia L. Bladdernut

36. Aceraceae

EA Acer campestre L. Hedge or English Maple
A Acer ginnala Maxim. Siberian Maple
Acer Negundo L. (*Negundo aceroides* Moench, *Negundo Negundo* Karst.) Box
    Elder, Ash-leaved Maple
Acer nigrum Michx. (*A. saccharum* var. *nigrum* Britt.) Black Sugar Maple
Acer pennsylvanicum L. (*A. striatum* Du Roi) Striped Maple or Moosewood
EA. Acer platanoides L. Norway Maple
EA Acer pseudoplatanus L. Sycamore Maple
Acer rubrum L. Red or Soft Maple
Acer saccharinum L. (*A. dasycarpum* Ehrh.) Silver or White Maple
Acer saccharum Marsh. (*A. saccharinum* Wang., *A. barbatum* Michx.) Sugar or Rock
    Maple
Acer spicatum Lamb. (*A. montanum* Ait.) Mountain Maple
EA Acer tataricum L. Tartarian Maple

37. Sapindaceae

Aesculus glabra Willd. Fetid or Ohio Buckeye
A. Aesculus Hippocastanum L. Horse-chestnut
Aesculus octandra Marsh. (*AE. flava* Ait., *AE. lutea* Wang.) Sweet or Yellow Buckeye

RHAMNALES
38. Rhamnaceae

Rhamnus alnifolia L'Her. Alder-leaved Buckthorn
Rhamnus caroliniana Walt. (*Frangula caroliniana* A. Gray) Carolina Buckthorn, Indian Cherry
E. Rhamnus cathartica L. Common Buckthorn
E. Rhamnus Frangula L. (*Frangula Alnus* Mill.) Glossy Buckthorn
Rhamnus lanceolata Pursh. Lance-leaved Buckthorn
Ceanothus americanus L. New Jersey Tea, Red-root
Ceanothus ovatus Desf. Smaller Red-root
Berchemia scandens (Hill.) Koch. Supple Jack

39. Vitaceae

Parthenocissus quinquefolia (L.) Planch. (*Ampelopsis quinquefolia* Michx., *Psedera quinquefolia* (L.) Greene) Virginia Creeper
A Parthenocissus tricuspidata (Sieb. and Zucc.) Planch. (*Ampelopsis tricuspidata* Sieb. and Zucc.) Boston Ivy, Japanese Ivy
Parthenocissus vitacea (Knerr) Hitchc. (*Psedera vitacea*) Virginia Creeper
Vitis aestivalis Michx. Summer or Pigeon Grape
Vitis argentifolia Muns. (*V. bicolor* Le Conte) Blue-leaf Grape
Vitis cinerea Engelm. (*V. aestivale* Michx. var. *cinerea* Engelm.) Sweet Winter Grape
Vitis Labrusca L. Northern Fox Grape
Vitis riparia Michx. (*V. vulpina* Authors not L.) Riverbank Grape

MALVALES
40. Tiliaceae

Tilia americana L. Basswood, Linden

Several other very similar and apparently little understood species have been described. For a treatment of these see Sargent's "Manual of Trees."

41. Malvaceae

A. Hibiscus syriacus L. (*Althaea frutex* Hort.) Rose of Sharon, Shrubby Althaea

42. Thymelaeaceae

E. Daphne Mezereum L. Mezereum
Dirca palustris L. Leatherwood or Wicopy

PARIETALES
43. Hypericaceae

Ascyrum stans Michx. St. Peter's-wort
Ascyrum hypericoides L. St. Andrew's Cross
Hypericum densiflorum Pursh. Shrubby St. John's-wort
Hypericum Kalmianum L. Kalm's St. John's-wort
Hypericum prolificum L. Shrubby St. John's-wort

44. Cistaceae

Hudsonia ericoides L. Heath-like Hudsonia
Hudsonia tomentosa Nutt. Woolly Hudsonia, False Heather

MYRTIFLORAE
45. Elaeagnaceae

EA Elaeagnus angustifolia L. Oleaster or Russian Olive
W Elaeagnus commutata Bernh. (*E. argentea* Pursh.) Silverberry

W   Shepherdia argentea Nutt. (*Lepargyraea argentea* (Wuth.) Greene) Silver Buffalo-
     berry
     Shepherdia canadensis (L.) Nutt. (*Lepargyraea canadensis* (L.) Greene) Russet
     Buffalo-berry

UMBELLIFLORAE
46. Araliaceae

A   Acanthopanax Sieboldianus Mak. (*Aralia pentaphylla* Thunb.) Spiny Panax
     Aralia hispida Vent. Bristly Sarsaparilla, Wild Elder
     Aralia spinosa L. Hercules Club
E.   Hedera Helix L. English Ivy

47. Nyssaceae
     Nyssa sylvatica Marsh. Sour Gum, Tupelo, Pepperidge

48. Cornaceae

EA   Cornus alba L. Siberian Dogwood
     Cornus alternifolia L.f. Alternate-leaved or Pagoda Dogwood
     Cornus Amomum Mill. (*C. sericea* L.) Silky Cornel or Kinnikinnik
     Cornus asperifolia Michx. Rough-leaved Dogwood
     Cornus florida L. (*Cynoxylon floridum* (L.) Raf.) Flowering Dogwood
EA   Cornus mas L. (*C. mascula* Hort.) Cornelian Cherry
     Cornus racemosa Lam. (*C. paniculata* L'Her.) Gray Dogwood
     Cornus rugosa Lamb. (*C. circinata* L'Her.) Round-leaved Dogwood
     Cornus stolonifera Michx. Red-osier Dogwood

ERICALES
49. Ericaceae

E.   Calluna vulgaris (L.) Hull. Heather
     Clethra acuminata Michx. Mountain Sweet Pepperbush
     Clethra alnifolia L. Sweet Pepperbush or White Alder
     Chimaphila maculata (L.) Pursh. Spotted Wintergreen
     Chimaphila umbellata (L.) Bart. Prince's Pine, Pipsissewa
     Ledum groenlandicum Oeder. Labrador Tea
     Rhododendron arborescens (Pursh) Torr. (*Azalea arborescens* Pursh) Smooth Azalea
     Rhododendron canadense (L.) Torr. (*Rhodora canadensis* L.) Rhodora
     Rhododendron canescens (Michx.) Sweet. (*Azalea canescens* Michx.) Piedmont
     Azalea
S   Rhododendron catawbiense Michx. Mountain Rose Bay
     Rhododendron lapponicum (L.) Wahl. (*Azalea lapponica* L.) Lapland Rhododendron
     Rhododendron maximum L. Great Laurel, Rose Bay
     Rhododendron nudiflorum (L.) Torr. (*Azalea nudiflora* L.) Pinkster-flower
     Rhododendron viscosum (L.) Torr. (*Azalea viscosa* L.) Swamp Pink, White Azalea
     Leiophyllum buxifolium (Berg.) Ell. (*Dendrium buxifolium* (Berg.) Ell.) Sand
     Myrtle
     Loiseleuria procumbens (L.) Desv. (*Chamaecistus procumbens* (L.) Ktze.) Alpine
     Azalea
     Kalmia angustifolia L. Sheep Laurel, Lambkill
     Kalmia latifolia L. Mountain Laurel
     Kalmia polifolia Wang. Pale Laurel
     Phyllodoce coerulea (L.) Bab. (*Bryanthus taxifolius* A. Gray) Mountain Heath
     Cassiope hypnoides (L.) D. Don
     Leucothoe racemosa (L.) Gray. Sweetbells
     Leucothoe recurva (Buckley) Gray
     Andromeda glaucophylla Link. Bog-rosemary
     Lyonia ligustrina (L.) DC. (*Xolisma ligustrina* (L.) Britt.)
     Lyonia mariana (L.) D. Don. (*Xolisma mariana* (L.) Rehd.)
     Chamaedaphne calyculata (L.) Moench. (*Cassandra calyculata* D. Don) Leather-leaf,
     Cassandra
     Oxydendrum arboreum (L.) DC. (*Andromeda arborea* L.) Sourwood, Sorrel-tree
     Epigaea repens L. Trailing Arbutus or Mayflower

Gaultheria procumbens L. Wintergreen
Arctostaphylos Uva-ursi (L.) Spreng. (*Uva-ursi Uva-ursi* (L.) Britt.) Bearberry
Chiogenes hispidula (L.) T. and G. (*C. serpyllifolia* Salisb.) Creeping Snowberry
Gaylussacia baccata (Wang.) K. Koch. Black Huckleberry
Gaylussacia brachycera (Michx.) A. Gray. Box Huckleberry
Gaylussacia dumosa (Andrews) T. and G. Dwarf Huckleberry
Gaylussacia frondosa (L.) T. and G. Blue Fangle, Dangleberry
Vaccinium arboreum Marsh. (*Batodendron arboreum* (Marsh.) Nutt.) Farkleberry,
    Tree-huckleberry
Vaccinium caespitosum Michx. Dwarf Bilberry
Vaccinium myrtilloides Michx. (*V. canadense* Rich.) Canada Blueberry
Vaccinium corymbosum L. High-bush or Tall Blueberry
Vaccinium corymbosum L. var. glabrum (Gray) Camp. High-bush Blueberry
Vaccinium macrocarpon Ait. (*Oxycoccus macrocarpus* (Ait.) Pursh.) Large Cranberry
Vaccinium Oxycoccus L. (*Oxycoccus Oxycoccus* (L.) MacMillan) Cranberry
Vaccinium angustifolium Ait. (*V. pennsylvanicum* Lamb.) Low Sweet Blueberry,
    Dwarf Blueberry
Vaccinium stamineum L. (*Polycodium stamineum* (L.) Greene) Deerberry
Vaccinium uliginosum L. Great or Bog Bilberry
Vaccinium vacillans Kalm. Late Low Blueberry
Vaccinium Vitis-Idaea L. (*Vitis-Idaea Vitis-Idaea* (L.) Britt.) Cranberry, Foxberry

EBENALES
50. Ebenaceae
Diospyros virginiana L. Common Persimmon

51. Styracaceae
S   Halesia carolina L. (*H. tetraptera* L., *Mohrodendron carolinum* Britt.) Snowdrop or
    Silver Bell Tree
CONTORTAE
52. Oleaceae
Chionanthus virginica L. Fringe Tree or Old Man's Beard
A   Forsythia intermedia Zabel. Border Forsythia
A   Forsythia suspensa Vahl. Weeping Forsythia
A   Forsythia viridissima Lindl. Golden Bell, Greenstem Forsythia
Fraxinus americana L. White Ash
EA   Fraxinus excelsior L. European Ash
Fraxinus nigra Marsh. (*F. sambucifolia* Lamb.) Black or Hoop Ash
Fraxinus pennsylvanica Marsh. (*F. pubescens* Lamb.) Red Ash
Fraxinus pennsylvanica Marsh. var. lanceolata (Borkh.) Sarg. (*F. viridis* Michx. f.)
    Green Ash
Fraxinus quadrangulata Michx. Blue Ash
Fraxinus tomentosa Michx. f. (*F. profunda*) Pumpkin Ash
A   Ligustrum ovalifolium Hassk. (*L. californicum* Hort.) California Privet
EA.   Ligustrum vulgare L. Common Privet
A   Ligustrum obtusifolium Sieb. and Zucc. (*L. Ibota* Sieb.)
A   Ligustrum obtusifolium var. Regelianum (Koehne) Rehd. Regel Privet.
E   Syringa vulgaris L. Common Lilac

53. Apocynaceae
E.   Vinca minor L. Periwinkle

TUBULIFLORAE
54. Verbenaceae
Callicarpa americana L. French or Bermuda Mulberry

55. Solanaceae
E.   Lycium halimifolium Mill. (*L. vulgare Dunal*) Matrimony Vine
E.   Solanum Dulcamara L. European Bittersweet, Bitter Nightshade

56. Scrophulariaceae

A. Paulownia tomentosa (Thunb.) Steudel. (*P. imperialis* Sieb. and Zucc.) Princess Tree

57. Bignoniaceae

S. Catalpa bignonioides Walt. (*C. Catalpa* Karst.) Common Catalpa
Catalpa speciosa Warder. Western Catalpa
Bignonia capreolata L. (*B. crucigera* L., in part) Trumpet-flower, Cross-vine
Campsis radicans Seem. (*Tecoma radicans* (L.) Juss., *Bignonia radicans* L.)
Trumpet-creeper, Trumpet-vine

RUBIALES
58. Rubiaceae

Cephalanthus occidentalis L. Button-bush
Mitchella repens L. Partridge Berry

59. Caprifoliaceae

Diervilla Lonicera Mill. (*D. trifida* Moench, *D. Diervilla* (L.) MacMillan) Bush
Honeysuckle
Linnaea borealis L. var. americana (Forbes) Rehd. Twinflower
Lonicera caerulea L. var. villosa Michx. Mountain Fly Honeysuckle
Lonicera canadensis Marsh. (*L. ciliata* Muhl.) American Fly Honeysuckle
Lonicera dioica L. (*L. glauca* Hill) Climbing Honeysuckle
Lonicera hirsuta Eaton. Hairy Honeysuckle
A. Lonicera japonica Thunb. Japanese Honeysuckle
E. Lonicera Morrowi Gray. Morrow Honeysuckle
Lonicera oblongifolia (Goldie) Hook. Swamp Fly Honeysuckle
Lonicera prolifera Rehd. (*L. sullivantii* Gray)
E. Lonicera sempervirens L. Trumpet Honeysuckle
A. Lonicera tatarica L. Tartarian Honeysuckle
E. Lonicera Xylosteum L. European Fly Honeysuckle
Sambucus canadensis L. Common Elder
Sambucus racemosa L. Red-berried Elder
Symphoricarpos albus (L.) Blake. (*S. racemosus* Michx.) Snowberry or Waxberry
Symphoricarpos orbiculatus Moench. (*S. vulgaris* Michx., *S. symphoricarpos* (L.)
MacMillan.) Coral Berry
Viburnum acerifolium L. Maple-leaved Arrow-wood, Dockmackie
Viburnum alnifolium Marsh. (*V. lantanoides* Michx.) Hobble-bush
Viburnum cassinoides L. (*V. nudum* var. *cassinoides* T. and G.) Withe-rod, Wild
Raisin
Viburnum dentatum L. Arrow-wood
EA. Viburnum Lantana L. Wayfaring-tree
Viburnum Lentago L. Sheep-berry, Nannyberry
Viburnum molle Michx. Soft-leaved Arrow-wood
Viburnum nudum L. Naked Withe-rod
EA Viburnum Opulus L. Snowball, European Cranberry-bush
Viburnum Opulus L. var. americanum (Mill.) Ait. (*V. trilobum* Marsh.) High-bush
Cranberry
Viburnum pubescens Pursh. (*V. venosum* Britt.)
Viburnum pauciflorum Raf. Squashberry, Pimbina
Viburnum prunifolium L. Black Haw.
Viburnum Rafinesquianum Schult. (*V. pubescens* Auth. not Pursh.) Downy Arrow-
wood
Viburnum rufidulum Raf.
Viburnum scabrellum (T. and G.) Chapm. (*V. semitomentosum* Rehd.)

CUCURBITALES
60. Compositae

Baccharis halimifolia L. Groundsel-tree
Iva frutescens L. (*I. oraria* Bartlett.) Marsh Elder, High-water Shrub

D. SOME PUBLICATIONS ON WOODY PLANTS

1. General Books

APGAR, A. C.—Trees of the Northern United States. New York, 1892. Keys, descriptions, and illustrations.

——————. Ornamental Shrubs of the United States. New York, 1910. Illustrations, descriptions, and keys to species.

BAILEY, L. H.—A Manual of Cultivated Plants. New York, 1949. A manual for the identification of our cultivated plants including woody plants; contains descriptions and keys for families, genera, and species.

——————. The Cultivated Conifers. New York, 1933. A general comprehensive treatment of conifers, including their cultivation, propagation, diseases, use, identification, etc.; successor to The Cultivated Evergreens, 1924.

——————, AND ETHEL ZOE BAILEY.—Hortus Second. New York, 1941. A concise dictionary of gardening, general horticulture, and cultivated plants in North America.

BRITTON, N. L.—North American Trees. New York, 1908. Like Sargent's Manual but less technical.

COLLINGWOOD, G. H., AND W. D. BRUSH.—Knowing Your Trees. Amer. Forestry Assoc., Washington, D.C., 1947.

CURTIS, CARLTON C., AND S. C. BAUSER.—The Complete Guide to North American Trees. New York, 1943.

DALLIMORE, W., AND A. B. JACKSON.—A Handbook of Coniferae. London, 1923. A nontechnical treatment of conifers in cultivation; contains keys, descriptions, illustrations, etc., also extensive bibliography.

EMERSON, ARTHUR I., AND C. M. WEED.—Our Trees, How to Know Them. New York, 1946.

HARLOW, W. M., AND E. S. HARRAR.—Textbook of Dendrology. New York, 1941.

JACQUES, H. E.—How to Know the Trees. Dubuque, Iowa, 1946.

KEELER, HARRIET L.—Our Native Trees and How to Identify Them. New York, 1929. Non-technical; descriptions and illustrations; no keys.

——————. Our Northern Shrubs and How to Identify Them. Ed. 2. New York, 1928. Like the above, but dealing with shrubs only.

MATHEWS, F. S.—Field Book of American Trees and Shrubs. New York, 1925. Descriptions, illustrations, and general information.

MUNNS, E. N.—The Distribution of Important Forest Trees of the United States. U.S.D.A. Misc. Publ. 287, 1938.

PRESTON, R. J., JR.—North American Trees. Ames, Iowa, 1948. Illustrations and descriptions of trees north of Mexico.

REHDER, ALFRED.—Manual of Cultivated Trees and Shrubs. Ed. 2. New York, 1940. A comprehensive treatment with keys, descriptions, and general information.

ROGERS, JULIA E.—The Tree Book. New York, 1935. A popular guide to North American trees; descriptions, illustrations, and discussions.

ROGERS, W. E.—Tree Flowers of Forest, Park and Street. The Author, Appleton, Wisc., 1935. Excellent illustrations and descriptions.

SARGENT, C. S.—Manual of Trees of North America. Ed. 2. Boston, 1933. Keys, descriptions, and ranges.

——————. Silva of North America. Boston, 1891–1902. Very extensive; illustrations, full descriptions, keys, etc.

SCHAFFNER, J. H.—Field Manual of Trees. Ed. 2. Columbus, 1922.

SCHNEIDER, C. K.—Dendrologische Winterstudien. Jena, 1903. Extensive descriptions and figures of many native and cultivated genera of Europe; keys to species.

——————. Illustriertes Handbuch der Laubholzkunde. Jena, 1906–1912. A very extensive work on the native and introduced plants of Europe; descriptions, keys, illustrations, etc.; includes many American species.

SUDWORTH, G. B.—Check List of the Trees of the United States. Their Names and Ranges. U.S.D.A. Misc. Circular 92, 1927.

TRELEASE, W.—Plant Materials of Decorative Gardening; The Woody Plants. Ed. 3. Urbana, 1926. Keys to genera and species; descriptions of genera.

————. Winter Botany. Ed. 2. Urbana, 1925. Keys, descriptions, and illustrations; nearly all of our cultivated forms are included.

UNITED STATES DEPARTMENT OF AGRICULTURE.—Trees: The Yearbook of Agriculture. Washington, D.C., 1949. An exhaustive volume on many phases of trees.

2. Northeastern States

BARRETT, MARY F.—A Field Key to the Genera of Wild and Cultivated Hardy Trees of the Northeastern U.S. and Canada. Bloomfield, N.J., 1931. Based upon summer condition; glossary.

BLAKESLEE, A. F., AND C. D. JARVIS.—New England Trees in Winter. Storrs Exp. Sta. (Conn.) Bull. 69, 1911. Keys, descriptions, and illustrations.

————. Trees in Winter. New York, 1931. The above in book form.

BROWN, H. P.—Trees of New York State, Native and Naturalized. New York State College of Forestry, Technical Publ. No. 15, Syracuse, 1921. Contains a general treatment of the morphology of the parts of trees; keys to species based upon (1) leaves, (2) twigs, (3) fruits; a full page illustration showing leaves, twigs, flowers, and fruits and a page of description are devoted to each species; much general information is also given.

————. Trees of Northeastern United States. Boston, 1938.

BURNS, C. P., AND C. H. OTIS.—The Trees of Vermont. Vermont Bull. 194, 1916. Keys, descriptions, and illustrations.

COLLINS, J. F., AND H. W. PRESTON.—Key to Trees. New York, 1912. Keys based on summer characteristics; illustrations of leaves and bark.

CURTIS, C. C.—A Guide to the Trees. New York, 1925. Keys, brief descriptions, and illustrations based upon the summer condition of the trees of northeastern United States.

DAME, L. L., AND H. BROOKS.—Handbook of the Trees of New England. Boston, 1904. Descriptions and illustrations.

GRAVES, A. H., AND H. M. RUSK.—A Teaching Guide to the Trees of Greater New York. The Authors, Brooklyn Botanic Garden, Brooklyn, 1933.

HOUGH, ROMEYN B.—Handbook of the Trees of the Northern States and Canada East of the Rocky Mountains. New York, 1947.

HUNTINGTON, A. L.—Studies of Trees in Winter. Boston, 1910. Descriptions and habit notes; illustrations of habit and bark; no keys.

HYLAND, F., AND F. H. STEINMETZ.—The Woody Plants of Maine. Orono, 1944. Annotated catalogue.

ILLICK, J. S.—Pennsylvania Trees. Penn. Dept. of Forestry Bull. 11, 1914. Illustrations, descriptions, comparisons, and summer and winter keys.

————. Tree Habits; How to Know the Hardwoods. Washington, D.C., 1924.

————. Common Trees of New York. Washington, D.C., 1927. A non-technical handbook of the common trees of New York.

LEAVITT, ROBERT G.—The Forest Trees of New England. Boston, 1933.

WIEGAND, K. M., AND F. W. FOXWORTHY.—A Key to Genera of Woody Plants in Winter. Ed. 3. Ithaca, 1908. Includes those genera containing species native or cultivated in New York State.

3. Central States

BILLINGTON, C.—Shrubs of Michigan. Cranbrook Inst. Sci. Bull. 20, 1944.

DEAM, C. C.—Trees of Indiana. Ind. Dept. of Conservation Publ. 13, ed. 4, Indianapolis,

1931. Contains keys to families, genera, and species; illustrations, distribution, and general information.

————. Shrubs of Indiana. Ind. Dept. of Conservation Publ. 44, ed. 2, Indianapolis, 1932. Contains keys to genera and species; illustrations, distribution, and general information.

GATES, F. C.—Handbook of Kansas Trees. In Report of Kans. Bd. of Agric. XLVII: No. 186a, 1928. Keys, descriptions, illustrations, and local distributions.

OTIS, C. H.—Michigan Trees. Univ. of Michigan Bull., ed. 4, Ann Arbor, 1920. Keys, descriptions, and illustrations.

POOL, R. J.—Handbook of Nebraska Trees. Nebr. Conservation and Soil Survey Bull. 7, Lincoln, 1920. Illustrations, non-technical descriptions, keys, distribution, etc.

ROSENDAHL, C. O., AND F. K. BUTTERS.—Trees and Shrubs of Minnesota. Minneapolis, 1928. Keys to families, genera, and species; descriptions, distribution, and many illustrations.

SHIMEK, B.—Keys to Woody Plants of Iowa. Ed. 2, rev. Iowa City, 1930.

TEHON, L. R.—Fieldbook of Native Illinois Shrubs. Ill. Nat. History Survey, Manual 3, 1942.

4. Southern United States and Mexico

BENSON, L., AND R. A. DARROW.—A manual of Southwestern Desert Trees and Shrubs. Univ. Ariz. Biol. Sci. Bull. 6, 1944. A comprehensive manual including keys to families, genera, and species; descriptions; illustrations, many in color; distribution maps; and glossary.

BERRY, J. B.—Southern Woodland Trees. Cleveland, 1924.

BROWN, CLAIR A.—Louisiana Trees and Shrubs. Louisiana Forestry Commission No. 1, 1945.

BUSWELL, W. M.—Native Trees and Palms of South Florida. Univ. of Miami Bull. 19, 1945. Keys and descriptions; some illustrations.

————. Native Shrubs of South Florida. Univ. of Miami Bull. Vol. 20: No. 3, 1946. Keys and descriptions; some illustrations.

COKER, W. C., AND W. R. TOTTEN.—Trees of the Southeastern States. Chapel Hill, 1945. Descriptions, illustrations, and keys.

DUNCAN, W. H.—Guide to Georgia Trees. Athens, Ga., 1941. Keys to genera and species.

FRIEND, W. H.—Plants of Ornamental Value for the Rio Grande Valley of Texas. Texas Agr. Exp. Sta. Bull. 609, College Station, 1942.

GILL, TOM.—Tropical Forests of the Central Caribbean. Tropical Plant Research Foundation, 1931.

GREEN, CHARLOTTE H.—Trees of the South. Chapel Hill, 1939. Photographs; popular descriptions; no keys.

HARPER, R. M.—Economic Botany of Alabama. Geol. Survey of Alabama Monograph 9, 1928. A catalogue of trees, shrubs, and vines, with their economic properties and local distribution; illustrations and references.

HARRAR, E. S., AND J. G. HARRAR.—Guide to the Southern Trees. New York, 1946.

MOWRY, HAROLD.—Ornamental Trees. Florida Agr. Exp. Sta. Bull. 261, 1933.

SMALL, J. K.—Florida Trees: A Handbook of the Native and Naturalized Trees of Florida. The Author, New York, 1913.

STANDLEY, P. C.—Trees and Shrubs of Mexico. Contr. U.S. Nat. Herbarium, Vol. 23, Washington, D.C., 1920. Keys, descriptions, and ranges.

5. Rocky Mountains

HAWKINS, P. H.—The Trees and Shrubs of Yellowstone National Park. Absarokee, Mont., 1924. A popular treatment.

KIRKWOOD, J. E.—Northern Rocky Mountain Trees and Shrubs. Stanford Univ., 1930. Keys to families, genera, and species; complete descriptions, distribution, and many illustrations.

LONGYEAR, B. O.—Trees and Shrubs of the Rocky Mountain Region. New York, 1927.

PRESTON, R. J.—Rocky Mountain Trees. Ames, Iowa, 1940. Descriptions, illustrations, maps, keys, and glossary.

THONE, F. E. A.—Trees and Shrubs of Yellowstone National Park. St. Paul, 1929.

6. Pacific Coast

BAILEY, VIRGINIA L., AND H. E. BAILEY.—Woody Plants of the Western National Parks. Notre Dame, Ind., 1949.

BENSON, G. T.—The Trees and Shrubs of Western Oregon. Contr. Dudley Herbarium of Stanford Univ. 2: 1–170, 1930. Contains keys to genera and species; distribution.

BOWERS, N. A.—Cone-bearing Trees of the Pacific Coast. New York, 1942. Compact field manual for native species.

ELIOT, W. A., AND G. B. McLEAN.—Forest Trees of the Pacific Coast. New York, 1938.

GRANT, JOHN A., AND CAROL L. GRANT.—Trees and Shrubs for Pacific Northwest Gardens. Seattle, 1943.

JEPSON, W. L.—Trees of California. San Francisco, 1909. Keys, descriptions, some illustrations, and much general information.

————. Silva of California. Univ. of Calif. Mem. No. 2, Berkeley, 1909. More technical than the above.

McMINN, H. E.—An Illustrated Manual of California Shrubs. San Francisco, 1939.

————, AND E. MAINO.—An Illustrated Manual of Pacific Coast Trees. Berkeley, 1946. Keys to genera and species; brief descriptions; illustrations; planting lists for ornamentals and shade trees; glossary.

SUDWORTH, G. B.—Forest Trees of the Pacific Coast. U.S. Forest Service Bull., 1908. Descriptions, illustrations, ranges, no keys; 150 forest trees treated.

TAYLOR, RAYMOND F.—Pocket Guide to Alaska Trees. U.S.D.A. Misc. Publ. 55, 1929.

7. Canada

GRIFFITH, B. G.—A Pocket Guide to the Trees and Shrubs of British Columbia. Victoria, B.C., 1934. Keys, descriptions, and ranges.

MORTON, B. R., AND R. G. LEWIS.—Native Trees of Canada. Canadian Dept. of Forestry Bull. 61, 1917. Descriptions, illustrations, comparative tables, and ranges.

WHITE, J. H.—The Forest Trees of Ontario. Toronto, 1925. Treats native and some introduced trees; keys; descriptions; illustrations of fruits, leaves, and twigs.

WHITFORD, H. N., AND R. D. CRAIG.—Forests of British Columbia. Conservation Commission of Canada, Ottawa, 1918. Contains a good treatment of the trees of this region; descriptions, illustrations, distribution, etc.

E. GLOSSARY

Accessory buds. Additional buds when more than one occurs in or near the axil: of two kinds, collateral or superposed.

Achene. Small, dry and hard, one-seeded indehiscent fruit.

Acicular. Needle-shaped.

Acuminate. Gradually tapering to a long point.

Acute. Sharp pointed.

Adnate. Congenital union of two different organs.

Aggregate fruit. One formed by the coherence of several pistils that were distinct in the flower.

Alternate. One (leaf or bud) at a node; placed singly at different heights on the stem.

Angiospermae. Plants with seeds borne in an ovary.

Anterior. The side away from the axis or stem.

Appressed. Lying close and flat against.

Arborescent. Tree-like, in size or form.

Ascending. Rising obliquely upwards.

Auriculate. Furnished with ear-like appendages.

Axil. Upper angle formed where the leaf joins the stem.

Axillary buds. Buds in or from an axil.

Berry. Fleshy fruit, soft throughout.

Biennial. Of two year's duration.

Blade. The expanded part of a leaf.

Bract. A reduced or modified leaf, usually below a flower.

Bracteole. A small bract.

Branchlet. An ultimate division of a branch, not including the last season's growth.

Bundle-scars. Scars formed in a leaf-scar by the breaking of the vascular bundles of the petiole.

Capsule. Dry, dehiscent fruit of a compound pistil.

Carinate. Having a keel or projecting longitudinal medial line on the lower or outer surface.

Chambered pith. Pith in transverse plates with air cavities between them.

Ciliate. Fringed with hairs on the margin.

Collateral buds. Accessory buds at the side of the main axillary bud.

Compound leaves. Those in which the blade consists of two or more separate parts (leaflets).

Conduplicate. Two parts folded lengthwise along the midrib.

Connate. Congenital union of like structures.

Convolute. Rolled up lengthwise.

Cordate. Heart-shaped.

Coriaceous. Of the texture of leather.

Corymb. A flat or convex flower cluster with the outer flower opening first.

Crenate. Dentate with the teeth much rounded.

Crenulate. Finely crenate.

Cuneate. Wedge-shaped.

Cuspidate. Tipped with a sharp and rigid point.

Cyme. A broad, more or less flat-topped flower cluster, with central flowers opening first.

Deciduous. Falling off in autumn.

De-compound. Several times compound or divided.

Decumbent. Reclining at base but the summit ascending.

Decurrent. Extending down the stem below the insertion.

Deliquescent. The main stem branching off into numerous smaller ones.

Deltoid. Triangular.

Dentate. Toothed, teeth pointing outward; (cf. serrate).

Denticulate. Furnished with minute teeth.

Depressed. Somewhat flattened from the end.

Dichotomous. Forking regularly by pairs.

Divaricate. Widely divergent or spreading.

Drupe. Fleshy stone fruit with inner part of wall bony and outer part soft.

Elliptical. Oval or oblong with the ends rounded.

Emarginate. With a shallow notch at the apex.

Entire. Margin even, not toothed, notched, or divided.

Ephemeral. Short lived.

Excurrent. The stem or trunk continuing to the top of the tree.

Exfoliating. Cleaving off in thin layers.

Exserted. Projecting beyond an envelope.

Falcate. Scythe-shaped.

Fastigiate (branches). Erect, near together and more or less parallel, in dense masses.

Floccose. With locks or bunches of soft or woolly hair.

Follicle. A fruit consisting of a single carpel splitting along the inner or upper suture only.

Fusiform. Spindle-shaped, swollen in the middle and tapering toward each end.

Glabrate. Somewhat glabrous, or becoming glabrous.

Glabrous. Without hairs.

Gland. A secreting part or appendage, but term often used for small swellings or projections on various organs.

Glandular. Furnished with glands, or gland-like.

Glaucous. Covered or whitened with a bloom.

Globose. Spherical in form or nearly so.

Globular. Nearly globose.

Glutinous. Sticky.

Granulose. Composed of or appearing as if covered by minute grains.

Gymnospermae. Plants with seeds borne naked.

Hastate. Shaped like an arrow-head but with the basal lobes spreading.

Head. A short compact flower cluster of more or less sessile flowers.

Herbaceous. Not woody; of the texture of an herb.

Hirsute. With rather coarse hairs.

Hispid. With rigid hairs or bristles.

Imbedded buds. Completely or partially sunken in the bark.

Imbricate. Overlapping like the shingles on a roof.

Inflorescence. Mode of flower bearing; a flower cluster.

Involucre. A whorl of small leaves or bracts standing close below a flower or flower cluster.

Lanceolate. Several times longer than wide, broadest near the base and narrowed to the apex.

Leaflet. One part of a compound leaf.

Leaf-scar. A scar left on the twig when a leaf falls.

Legume. Dehiscent dry fruit of a simple pistil normally splitting along two sides.

Lenticel. A small corky area or speck serving as a breathing pore.

Ligulate. Strap-shaped.

Linear. Long and narrow with parallel margins.

Lobed. Divided into segments about to the middle.

Lunate. Crescent-shaped, like the new moon.

Membranous. Thin, rather soft, and somewhat translucent.

Mucronate. Furnished with an abrupt minute point.

Multiple fruit. One formed by the coherence of pistils and associated parts of the several flowers of an inflorescence.

Netted venation. The principal veins of a leaf forming a network.

Node. A joint or place where leaves are attached to a stem.

Nut. A hard indehiscent one-celled and one-seeded fruit usually resulting from a compound ovary.

Nutlet. A small nut.

Oblanceolate. Like lanceolate, but with the narrow end towards the stem.

Oblique (leaves). Unequal sided.

Oblong. Longer than broad, and with the sides nearly parallel most of their length.

Obovate. Inverted ovate.

Obtuse. Blunt or rounded at the end.

Opposite. Two (leaves or buds) at a node.

Orbicular. Circular.

Ovate. Of the shape of a hen's egg with the broad end toward the base.

Palmate. Radiating fan-like from approximately one point.

Panicle. An elongated irregularly branched inflorescence.

Pappus. The modified calyx-limb in *Compositae*, forming a crown of various character at the summit of the achene.

Parallel venation. The principal veins of a leaf running parallel or nearly so.

Pedicel. Stem of an individual flower of a flower cluster.

Peduncle. Stem of a solitary flower or of a flower cluster.

Pellucid. Clear, nearly transparent.

Peltate. Attached to its stalk inside the margin; shield-shaped.

Pendulous. More or less hanging or declined.

Perennial. Of three or more season's duration.

Perfoliate. The stem appearing to pass through the leaf.

Persistent. Remaining attached; leaves not all falling off at the same time.

Petiole. The stalk of a leaf.

Pinnate. Arranged featherlike on each side of a common axis.

Plicate. Folded into plaits, usually lengthwise, like a closed fan.

Pome. Fleshy fruit with bony or leathery several-celled core and soft outer part.

Prickle. A small, sharp outgrowth from the bark or rind.

Prostrate. Lying flat upon the ground.

Pseudo-terminal bud. The uppermost lateral bud, on a twig lacking a terminal bud, appearing as a terminal bud. The terminal bud-scar with its ring of vascular tissue, and the axillary position of the bud will enable one to determine this condition.

Puberulent. Minutely pubescent.

Pubescent. Covered with soft, short hairs.

Raceme. A simple flower cluster of pedicelled flowers upon a common elongated axis.

Reniform. Kidney-shaped.

Retuse. With a shallow notch at a rounded apex.

Revolute. Rolled backwards from the margins or apex.

Rhachis. The axis of a spike or compound leaf.

Rugose. Wrinkled; generally due to the depression of the veins in the upper surface of the leaf.

Rugulose. Slightly wrinkled.

Sagittate. Shaped like an arrowhead; triangular, with the basal lobes pointing downward.

Samara. An indehiscent winged fruit.

Scabrous. Rough to the touch.

Scurfy. Covered with small bran-like scales.

Serrate. Having sharp teeth pointing forward.

Serrulate. Finely serrate.

Sessile. Without a stalk.

Simple leaves. Those in which the blade is all in one piece.

Sinus. The space or recess between two lobes of a leaf.

Spatulate. Gradually narrowed downward from a rounded summit.

Spike. A flower cluster like a raceme, but with sessile flowers.

Spine. A sharp, rather slender, rigid outgrowth.

Spur. A short, slowly-grown branchlet.

Stalked bud. One in which the outer scales are attached above the base.

Stellate. Star-shaped.

Stipel. Stipule of a leaflet.

Stipule. A basal appendage of a petiole, (usually two).

Stoloniferous. Bearing runners or shoots that take root.

Striate. Marked with fine longitudinal lines or ridges.

Strigose. With appressed, sharp, straight and stiff hairs.

Sub. A prefix meaning somewhat.

Subcordate. Slightly cordate.

Subulate. Awl-shaped; broad at base, narrow and tapering from the base to a sharp, rigid point, the sides generally concave.

Suffrutescent. Slightly or obscurely shrubby.

Superposed buds. Accessory buds above the axillary bud.

Supra-axillary. Located above an axil.

Tendril. A thread-like leaf or stem part by which a plant may cling to a support.

Terete. Round in cross-section.

Terminal bud. The bud formed at the tip of a twig.

Thorn. A degenerated, sharp pointed branch.

Tomentose. Densely hairy with matted wool.

Tomentulose. Slightly hairy with matted wool.

Trifoliate. Of three leaflets.

Truncate. Ending abruptly as if cut off transversely.

Twig. A young shoot: used to denote the growth of the past season only.

Umbel. An umbrella-like flower cluster.

Undulate. With a wavy margin or surface.

Valvate. Scales of the bud meeting by the edges and not overlapping.

Whorled. Three or more (leaves or buds) at a node.

TERMS USED TO DESCRIBE LEAVES

Generalized simple leaf: 1, b, blade; c, stipule; p, petiole; a, leaf axil; n, node; i, internode.

Arrangement: 2, alternate (spiral); 3, opposite; 4, whorled.

Composition: 5, simple; 6, pinnately compound; 7, palmately compound; 8, trifoliate; 9, decompound.

Venation: 10, parallel; 11, pinnately netted; 12, palmately netted.

Lobing: 13, pinnately lobed; 14, palmately lobed.

Margin: 15, entire; 16, serrate; 17, dentate; 18, crenate; 19, undulate; 20, ciliate; 21, doubly-serrate.

Outline: 22, acicular; 23, linear; 24, lanceolate; 25, oblanceolate; 26, ovate; 27, obovate; 28, oblong; 29, elliptical; 30, deltoid; 31, orbicular; 32, subulate.

Apex: 33, acuminate; 34, acute; 35, obtuse; 36, truncate; 37, mucronate; 38, cuspidate; 39, emarginate; 40, retuse.

Base: 41, acuminate; 42, cuneate; 43, acute; 44, obtuse; 45, oblique; 46, cordate; 47, truncate; 48, auriculate; 49, sagittate; 50, hastate.

TERMS USED TO DESCRIBE
INFLORESCENCES AND WINTER BUDS

Inflorescences: 1, spike; 2, raceme; 3, corymb; 4, head; 5, panicle; 6, cyme; 7, umbel; 8, ament (catkin).

Buds: 9, terminal; 10, lateral; 11, pseudo-terminal; 23, clustered terminal.

Attitude of buds: 18, divaricate; 19, appressed.

Position of buds: 21, axillary; 16, superposed; 17, collateral.

Insertion of buds: 21, sessile; 22, stalked; 24, sub-petiolar.

Bud-scales: 20, valvate; 21, imbricate; 25, absent (naked bud).

Scars: 12, abscission scar of growing point; 14, terminal bud-scar; 15, pseudo-terminal bud-scar; 13, upper leaf-scar; 27, leaf-scar; 26, stipule-scar; 28, bundle-scar.

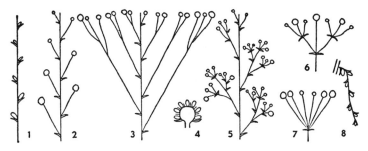

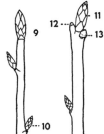

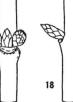

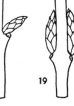

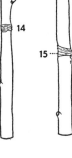

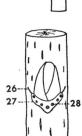

F. INDEX

(Synonyms are in italics)

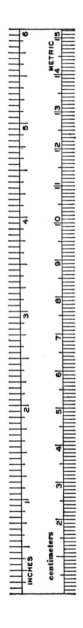